Spilling the T

GENDER TRANSITION,
BEYOND THE PHYSICAL

JAMES BENNETT

This book is a memoir reflecting the author's present recollections of experiences over time. Its story and its words are the author's alone. Some names, details, and characteristics may be changed, some events may be compressed, and some dialogue may be recreated.

Published by River Grove Books
Austin, TX
www.rivergrovebooks.com

Copyright © 2024 James Bennett

All rights reserved.

Thank you for purchasing an authorized edition of this book and for complying with copyright law. No part of this book may be reproduced, stored in a retrieval system, or transmitted by any means, electronic, mechanical, photocopying, recording, or otherwise, without written permission from the copyright holder.

Distributed by River Grove Books

Design and composition by Greenleaf Book Group and Mimi Bark
Cover design by Greenleaf Book Group and Mimi Bark
Cover images used under license from ©Shutterstock.com/photo4passion.at

Publisher's Cataloging-in-Publication data is available.

Print ISBN: 978-1-63299-891-0

eBook ISBN: 978-1-63299-892-7

First Edition

Dedicated to
Mom, Dad, and Lauren

The Goods

Preface   vii

1 | Lady in the Red Dress   1

2 | The LA Therapist   19

3 | Blue Island in a Sea of Red   35

4 | Departure of the Arch Nemeses   49

5 | The Juice   67

6 | Coming Out, Again   79

7 | The Australia Tattoo   89

8 | Jasmine's Lyft   101

9 | Male Impersonator   113

SPILLING THE T

10 | Dirty Jers' 123

11 | A Botched Goodbye 143

12 | One of Us 159

13 | The Vomit Carpet 175

14 | The Pita Chip Man 187

15 | Eggs before Easter 207

Conclusion 221

Acknowledgments 225

About the Author 227

Preface

I wish I had kept a tally of the number of times I have been asked about "The Surgery" since starting my transition in 2015. There would be a ton of little black lines on that page. Considering I present as a mostly typical male when clothed, what I have in my pants becomes the focal point of my entire existence once it becomes known I am transgender. *The penis in the room, if you will.* Five minutes prior, I was just James, and suddenly, I'm a confusing body with a giant question mark between my legs. My gender identity doesn't make sense to a staggeringly large percentage of the population without this crucial question answered. There are the occasional kind souls who don't ask, but the inevitable tension remains. I watch as they shake internally under the pressure, wanting so badly to have all of their questions answered. Is he a *real* man?

For those who do ask, the question is typically preceded by a strangely specific circular hand motion before their mouth forms the words I wish they wouldn't. They pause for a short period of time in the middle of a seemingly normal conversation, then look down before they motion toward the lower half of my body with their left or right hand, depending on dominance. The motion generally involves the index and middle finger, both pointed straight out while the two remaining fingers are curled inward toward the palm. The thumb usually isn't involved. They follow the hand motion with something along the lines of, "So what's the deal with . . ." or "Have you . . . ?" Their sentence then fades off without the question ever being completed.

I dream of the day that the majority of people ask me about anything else, preferably something of actual importance. The substance, the life shit. I want to talk of the ups and downs and all that I've learned about our society while morphing from one gender to another. I want to laugh about the time when I, a grown man, asked for women's size eight shoes at a rock-climbing gym or how I responded to the TSA agent who asked me, "Are you going through some kind of surgery or something?" I want to share how many times I've gotten the questions "Which way?" or "From what?" after telling someone I transitioned. I want it to be known how painful it is to be part of a community that no longer recognizes you and how impossibly difficult it is to learn how to interact with cisgender, straight men twenty-five years too late. Simply put, I long for a reality that does not exist.

As of today, we live in a world of penises and vaginas, and unfortunately, there isn't much I can do about that. So, instead of spending the rest of my life desperately longing, I decided

Preface

I will just pretend. I will pretend that the general population has asked or cares about anything other than my genitals, and I will write down my responses in the form of a book. The story nestled among these pages provides insight into gender transition, beyond the physical, spanning three states, two career moves, and marriage to an incredible woman who happens to share my birth name. For ease of navigation, I have included the symbol below at the beginning of each chapter in which my genitals are relevant. I imagine it will be surprising to many to see how few there really are.

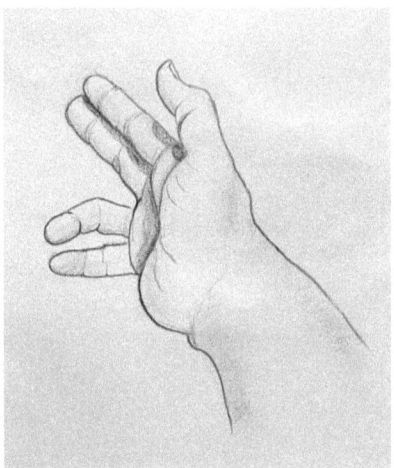

CHAPTER 1

Lady in the Red Dress

Roughly fifteen years before injecting hormones into my right thigh for the first time, I was on an afternoon walk with my dad in our new home, America. Mom had stayed behind at the extended stay hotel with my younger brother to add an additional hour to our *Animal Planet* marathon. The four of us were in awe of the sheer number of channels American TV had, and *Animal Planet* was like nothing we had ever seen. Australian TV offered vastly inferior, limited options. America in general felt like an expansive wonderland in comparison to our previous home. There were endless attractions to explore, and Dad and I were ready for some fresh air on this beautiful Sunday. He and I had always been the more adventurous two. We kissed Mom and Jonathan goodbye and ventured out to soak in Los Angeles through my enthusiastic ten-year-old eyes.

As we strolled down the sidewalk, I couldn't help but feel

excited. America was so busy and there was so much to see. We spoke of our new life and how my parents' company would prosper in the so-called "land of opportunity." Mom and Dad had recently sold their chain of arcades, once sprinkled up the east coast of Australia, and were looking for a new venture. Dad had been contacted by a man who proposed he travel over and set up a sprawling new venue near Los Angeles. Our family would then relocate roughly six months later, stay for two years while my dad built out the facility, sell said facility, and then return home to the motherland. I was filled to the brim with eagerness. I loved when Dad spoke of their business with me. It made me feel important and intelligent.

I smiled to myself as we walked, head in the clouds, when suddenly, something beautiful caught my eye. She was tall, maybe 5'9" or 5'10", curvy yet fit, and had luscious wavy, long brown hair. Her dress was red and came down at an angle over her knees. There was a strange pull inside of me as I watched her glide across the street with a gracious, confident elegance. My stomach danced with an increasing force with each step she took, my mind in disarray. I turned to my dad, eager for answers. I had seen many women in my life, yet somehow, this felt different. *Why?* Surely he could explain this foreign pitter-patter in my stomach.

"Dad, is it normal to be attracted to other women?" I cautiously asked. I worried that he would be confused by my peculiar, seemingly out-of-the-blue question. He paused briefly, then stopped and turned to me, hiding his surprise well. "Of course, darling, most women go through that phase," he responded reassuringly. This was all just part of the typical stages of development, he explained. My mind raced in response. There was nothing about this feeling that felt "typical." Up until that moment, I had been convinced that my dad knew everything, and suddenly, it became clear that he most definitely didn't. *How could both of these things be happening on the same day?* Not only was my dad wrong for the first time, I still couldn't explain the way I felt about the lady in the red dress. Falling asleep that night was no easy feat.

My life had been much simpler before that moment. "Oy, stay away from the colored ones," my dad used to say, warning my brother and me to be wary of all the venomous snakes and spiders that inhabited our expansive backyard in Australia. Jonathan and I spent most of our younger years outside, catching lizards and boogie boarding across the grass after it rained heavily. When it was time to come inside for meals, we would steal morsels of meat from the dinner table and leave them out for our toy dinosaurs. The herd was alive, and we were the only ones who knew it. Truthfully, blissful is the best word to describe my childhood.

The only inconvenience I faced day to day was contending with my mom's wardrobe choices for me. I hated when she put me in dresses or placed anything on my body that involved flowers or butterflies. I would pull on the fabric from all angles and simply exclaim, "Uncomfortable!" Mom quickly got the message, and those items eventually exited my wardrobe. My desire was to be clad like my brother in a simple T-shirt and shorts, so that's what we settled on. Neither of my parents were all that concerned at the time. I was a tomboy, and that wasn't necessarily unique for a young girl. My parents had friends with young daughters who liked "boy" things or sons who occasionally wanted to dress up like princesses. There was no need to define any of it at that age. No one even questioned my desire to be the husband when my cousins, brother, and I played house.

I had been able to mostly ignore the feelings brought up by the lady in the red dress until another event, about four years later, signaled that something wasn't quite right. It was my first marching band performance, I was geared up to go out on the football field in my spanking new uniform, and I chose to stop for one last pee beforehand. We were going to be out there for a while beating our drums and tooting our horns, and my bladder was a small one. I pulled down my bulky pants, sat down, and anxiously thought about my upcoming performance. As my stream came to a close, I looked down at my underwear before pulling them up and was greeted by a horrifying, foreign sight. Blood. My mind raced. *Was it cancer? Was I dying?* I somehow had not once considered prior to that day that I would eventually get my period. I knew what menstruation was, but the acknowledgment had ended there. I was bursting with newfound distress as I ran to the nurse's office.

The kind, older lady reassured me that I was, in fact, not dying and proceeded to teach me how to use a pad. I was mortified. *Was I really destined to do this for the better part of my life?* I returned to the bathroom, attempted to install the thick white apparatus onto my underwear, pulled up my heavy black pants, and ventured out onto the field. The excitement of my first performance had been replaced with a sense of severe dread. I would soon have to face what had happened in its totality, and I couldn't stand the thought.

After arriving home following the performance, I stood at the bottom of the stairs crying as my parents and I yelled back and forth. I suddenly hated everything, and I didn't know why. "This is exciting. You're a woman now!" my mom exclaimed with immense enthusiasm. I cried and screamed back at her, "I don't want to be a woman!" The downhill spiral had officially begun. No more uninterrupted bliss.

A year or so later, I sat my parents down for a "talk" at our kitchen table. Life had gotten increasingly more confusing: I still didn't like being a woman, and the "phase" was going strong. I had to let them in on it. I stared straight down as I anxiously curled and uncurled one of our placemats. "Stop it, Lauren!" my mom abruptly exclaimed. She couldn't stand when I played with the placemats. I looked up at both of them, their eyes filled with eagerness. "I think I'm bisexual," I said as an indescribable weight lifted off my shoulders. I had known I was attracted to women since that day in LA with Dad, and it was impossible that "normal" girls felt the same way I did. I couldn't hide behind the tomboy identity any longer. I had no interest in dating boys, and I was envious that my brother didn't have the same expectation. It wasn't for me, just as it wasn't for him. My mom and dad didn't need the intimate details to understand.

My mind flashed back briefly for a second to my first boyfriend. We were together for two weeks at the end of freshman year, and I hated most of it. One afternoon, we had been sitting on the floor watching a movie when he gently moved his hand over mine. I looked down to acknowledge the gesture and my eyes caught the outline of a certain something in his jeans. I was repulsed. There was no part of me that wanted to be close to that part of him. A few similar circumstances followed with different boys in the months after, and none of it ever felt natural to me. I shook my head to spin away the disgusting thoughts and focused back on the conversation with my parents.

As expected, they took the news well. My parents had never been the bigoted, homophobic type, and I was thankful for that. I didn't have to face the fear of rejection or disownment that is the reality for so many of my LGBTQ+ counterparts. My parents were admittedly still hopeful that I would end up with a boy, and at the time, I couldn't help but share the same sentiment. *Everything would eventually fall into place, right?* I craved for my life to be "normal."

After coming out to my parents, at the very least, I finally felt I had permission to venture out into the world of dating girls. It wasn't necessarily up to them, but it was reassuring that my mom and dad were at least on board with the idea. I wanted so badly to experience the feeling girls spoke of when they dated boys. It didn't matter to me that those feelings might be garnered from an individual of the same gender.

Within months, I finally felt the intoxicating concoction of nerves, dopamine overload, and unrelenting excitement others had spoken of. I found myself intertwined with my study buddy turned unrequited love, Rachel. She and I had met in our social studies class and connected on a shared inability to handle our teacher's caricature-like personality. Ms. Thatcher was loud, animated, and wore absurdly coordinated outfits with matching glue-like lipstick that made it hard to concentrate when she talked. She turned into a walking American flag around the Fourth of July. Rachel and I were constantly separated in class on account of our boisterous laughter.

Outside of school, we attempted to teach ourselves the topics we had missed, our study sessions quickly turning into what felt like a full-on relationship. We'd spend our afternoons at the beach, evenings at parties, and nights tangled up in steamy sleepovers. "Welcome back," the IHOP staff would say every Saturday morning, smiling as they seated us in *our* booth. My young heart fell quickly, and I was devastated when Rachel responded, "But I'm not gay," after I confessed my love to her. I briefly considered driving my car off the road on my way home, my eyes blurry with tears.

Following the smashing heartbreak, I spent a few lonely months listening to NSYNC's "Tearin' Up My Heart" on repeat until I found someone who gave me hope again. It all started on a night like so many during my latter teenage years—my friends and I, sans Rachel, drinking at a house party while some kid's parents were out of town. *My apologies, random parents.* I was drunk and scanning the party in an attempt to refocus my spinning eyes. It would be many more years before I learned the art of pacing my drinking. As I glanced around at the partygoers, my eyes landed on a girl across the room that halted my vision to immediate stability. From the moment I saw her, I couldn't stop staring. She was tall and slender with dark brown hair, and she was the most beautiful girl I had ever seen. Even prettier than the lady in the red dress.

I walked toward this exquisite creature, mustering up my courage with assistance from the liquid kind. "Hey, you're hot, I'm bi. My name is Lauren," I said to her, coupled with a coy smile. Her friends looked freaked out, but she responded with laughter, clearly flattered. The sweet sound was music to my ears, her friends quickly fading into the background. I didn't care what they thought. I was unable to focus on anything other than this girl's calming green eyes as they closed ever so slightly when she smiled back at me.

We spoke for a few minutes, surrounded by unwanted distraction, before we mutually decided to move away from the crowd. I slid open the glass door in the living room and ushered Carrie out into the dimly lit backyard ahead of me. The perimeter of the space was lined with tiki torches, their stands wedged deeply into the ground. Her eyes met mine briefly before we both headed for an unattended table situated privately in the back left corner of the yard. I could feel her electric energy next to me as we walked toward our shared refuge away from the noise, her sweet perfume streaming forcefully into my nostrils. My heart pounded with an unprecedented force as we weaved through the small clusters of people patched about the grass. I anxiously hoped that she hadn't picked up on how nervous I was.

We sat together for hours sharing our stories, adjusting our plastic chairs every so often as they sank into the wet grass. I fixated on how her lips moved, and the way her neck curved down to a part of her I dared to imagine I might touch one day. I grew distracted with her fingers as she drew them up to her mouth, a cigarette between them. They were long and slender, and I momentarily sensed how they would feel tracing down my body. I did all I could to listen intently to each word that she said, pushing away my early fantasies.

Carrie spoke of her family, her on-and-off-again asshole boyfriend, Timmy, and her job selling magazines door to door. She told me of her track record of top sales monthly, and I was impressed at the courage she must possess to do such a job. I could never walk up to a stranger's house and offer a product for sale. A wave of worry suddenly overtook me as I pictured it. *What if something happened to her?* She was a young, dangerously gorgeous girl coming awfully close to a door that could easily close behind her after one slight tug inward. There were a lot of scary men out in the world, and I didn't trust them. *Stop it, Lauren. Pay attention.* I forced myself back to the present moment. *Carrie will be fine.*

After what felt like an eternity, yet somehow still not long enough, Carrie and I agreed it was time to head home. It was nearing 2am, and we had school the next day. Most of the partygoers had already departed, and we were the only ones left in the backyard. I ran my fingers through the dew on the tabletop as I looked at her, desperate for the first kiss I hoped would come sooner rather than later. I was sure I should wait. I couldn't rush this thing and risk screwing it up. We headed back inside then stood on the driveway staring at each other, caught in a prolonged eye contact goodbye. The all-consuming kind in which you both refuse to break the iris connection. I didn't want the night to end, and I could sense that she felt the same. Carrie was "straight," but that didn't matter. This felt different from how things were with Rachel. Carrie was clearly into me, and I, her. My soul had been set on fire that night, and I would do anything to keep it alight.

The next few months were a whirlwind of emotions, firsts, and learning how to navigate the problematic behavior of some of those around us. My friends were enthusiastically on board with my new relationship, but separating from Carrie's prior friend group didn't come so easily. They were confused that she had suddenly "become a lesbian," and the ex-boyfriend, Timmy, was angered on account of his damaged ego. His eyes followed me with burning disdain when I passed him in the hall at school. I was thankful that he wasn't able to initiate a physical altercation with me. I was a girl, and boys weren't allowed to fight girls. *Lucky me.*

On a few occasions, Timmy and his friends would hurl the word "dyke" at me when I passed them at Starbucks, mocha Frappuccino in hand, but these interactions left me mostly unphased. It was my senior year, I was dating the prettiest girl in school, and they were just jealous. I felt an unexplainable struggle when I focused too heavily on Timmy's beautiful, quarterback-type frame, but the feelings quickly dissipated when I remembered that Carrie had chosen me over him. It didn't matter that I wasn't 6'3" with bulging muscles and washboard abs. I was me, and that was enough for her. A growing pride in my new identity slowly started to form. *Maybe being a woman isn't so bad after all?*

Young love

My parents embraced our new relationship with open arms and over time, slowly let go of the hope that I would end up with a boy. It didn't look like that was going to happen after all. I hadn't mentioned a single boy's name in months, except maybe Timmy and his abrasive friends, and Carrie and I were falling for each other quickly. We spent the majority of our time alone at Carrie's mom's apartment in the beginning, exploring our connection each afternoon. Carrie's mom, Davina, didn't work from home like my parents did, so we had many unattended hours after school, just the two of us. My fantasies from our first backyard meet turned out to be close to reality, and I was overwhelmed by how Carrie made me feel. We were going to be together forever—I was sure of it.

The only unknown was Davina's pending reaction. Neither of us were sure if she would accept that her daughter was now dating a woman. She and Carrie had never even discussed the possibility. At first, I would leave before Davina got home, but eventually, I began to stay on Tuesdays for their family favorite, beef tacos with ketchup. (Honestly, don't judge it before you try it.) One night after I left, Carrie called me to relay a conversation that she had just had with her mom. Davina had rightly caught on to the possibility that her daughter and I might be more than friends. My identity was no secret, and the two of us were spending an awful lot of time together. "It's okay if you and Lauren are more than friends," Davina had reassured Carrie as they cleaned up the taco remnants together. "I just hope you feel comfortable enough to tell me," she continued invitingly. I was ecstatic at the notion that Carrie's mom would be as supportive as my parents were. Carrie and I celebrated in shared relief, both grinning ear to ear on either side of the phone.

A week or so later, we agreed that it was finally time to let her mom in on our relationship status. Carrie sat Davina down, just the two of them, expecting to be met with the same warmth as their prior conversation. Unexpectedly, instead of responding to the news with the welcoming embrace we anticipated, Davina flipped out. All of the unknowingly feigned support was painfully rescinded, and Carrie called me bawling on account of the jolting shift. Her mom wasn't on board and apparently didn't agree with us being an item after all.

"Are you kidding me?" I practically screamed through the phone.

"No, I don't understand," Carrie said, sobbing with palpable pain in her voice.

I paced back and forth in my bedroom, throwing things intermittently in an attempt to counter my frustration. "I promise you we will sort this out," I told her. "Don't talk to your mom anymore about this, okay?"

Carrie was quiet for a few moments. "Okay, I love you," she said back.

"I love you too. I'll see you at school tomorrow." I preemptively decided to skip Tuesday dinner for a few weeks to let things settle down. I was still too angry, and I couldn't ruin my relationship with Davina if Carrie and I had any hope of rewriting the narrative of her support.

As I walked to my car after leaving Carrie's a few days later, I felt the presence of another pulling up behind me, a little too close for comfort. I pressed onward at a pace faster than my usual stroll, unable to muster up the courage to look behind me. My parking bay couldn't come soon enough. I heard a window roll down just as my hand met my car's door handle. My heart dropped as I heard Davina's voice. She had come home early.

"What are you, afraid of me?" she called out accusingly.

HERE WE GO, my brain screamed. I took a deep breath and whirled around, making eye contact with her through the dirty, bug-splattered windshield of her gold Camry. I walked up to the window, staring her down angrily as I drew closer. Carrie watched helplessly from their apartment's doorway, clearly concerned about what was going to happen.

"Not at all, Davina. I just can't believe how you've handled this situation," I borderline yelled back at her. "You lulled Carrie into a false sense of security, encouraging her to come out, only to unfairly retract all support when it became real."

Davina looked down, pressed with an inability to respond with any legitimate clarity. "It wasn't like that, Lauren. I was just kind of shocked."

While we feuded back and forth in the hot parking lot, the decibels in our voices slowly decreased as we began to find clarity. Davina wasn't going to say it, although I don't believe it was for lack of wanting to. She just hadn't yet found the words. It hit me that accepting the notion of a bisexual or lesbian daughter is probably much easier than embracing the reality that said daughter is actually *with* another woman. The life she had imagined for Carrie was suddenly being rewritten in a light she maybe hadn't truly comprehended prior. Things were going to be different, and she just needed time to adjust. This was new to everyone; we were all doing our best. Davina and I slowly came to a healthier place, with many words absent from the conversation, yet enough said to bring peace to the situation. She did accept Carrie and me, and we collectively agreed to remain communicative moving forward.

The three of us eventually returned to our delicious taco dinners, the tension mostly subsiding over the next few months. The end of my senior year quickly approached, and I was soon moving my life up to Santa Barbara for the first of four years at UCSB. Carrie still had a year left of high school, and that meant I was alone for the first time my young mind could remember. Carrie and I had spent almost every waking moment together since we met, and I felt lost without her. I was suddenly unsure of myself in a way that I had forgotten was possible. At home, everyone knew I liked women, but at college, no one knew anything about me. I didn't look like a stereotypical lesbian (yet), and I had no idea how to tell people I had a girlfriend. I attempted to forge a few friendships during orientation, but it all felt oddly out of character. I clicked initially with a friendly, outgoing girl from Georgia, but quickly grew consumed with worry of what she would think if I left out this crucial fact of my identity for too long. I would be considered deceitful and creepy, and possibly be shunned by others after she shared with them what I had done. There was seemingly no right way to go about it. I was overwhelmed, uncomfortable, and isolated.

A few weeks after the stressful orientation, I was in my new dorm, sitting at a wooden, built-in desk next to the smallest bed I had ever seen. I wondered how Carrie and I were ever going to sleep comfortably together in this ridiculous twin bed. Her visit the following weekend couldn't come fast enough. As I fantasized about our upcoming time together, I heard a knock at the door. I looked up, and my eyes were met by a shorter, sweet looking girl soon to share this 300-square-foot space with me. I was comforted, initially, by her presence before I noticed the glaring silver letters plastered across her black shirt: "GOD'S IMAGE." I had so many questions. *Is "GOD'S IMAGE" some sort of self-proclamation? Or is it the name of an actual group of people doing religious things together?* I had never seen anything like it.

Within a few minutes of our introduction, my new roomie

informed me that she planned to travel home to LA every weekend to sing in her choir group, God's Image. I lit up at the news. I now knew what God's Image was, and her absence meant that Carrie and I would be alone every weekend she visited. *Perfect.* In another twist of good fate, my roomie's absence also meant that I wouldn't have to come out to her. Religious folks were typically not okay with same-sex anything, so not having to explain my relationship with Carrie seemed pretty damn ideal. Things were looking up.

Settling in over the next few months mostly went off without a hitch. Classes were difficult but doable, and I slowly navigated telling everyone besides my religious roommate about my relationship. The Georgia peach from orientation shied away from me after I told her, but everyone else seemed generally okay with it, much to my surprise. I made new friends and grew closer to those from high school who were also attending UCSB. Carrie visited often, and our relationship continued on the same trajectory of soulmates destined for a lifetime of inseparable happiness. Freshman year was all roses until one major road bump with my roomie.

As was the case with any other Friday, my roomie had gone to the train station early to head home for the weekend. Shortly after, I picked Carrie up from that same station. We quickly hurried back to my dorm for our heavily anticipated reunion. *We hadn't seen each other in a whole seven days!* Unexpectedly, on this particular Friday, my roomie returned to the room to retrieve something she had forgotten. I knew the moment I heard the door unlatch that we were screwed. *No pun intended.*

I had never intended to come out to anyone this way, especially her. I was naked, on top of a very naked Carrie, with my bare ass facing the front door of the room. This was the worst-case scenario.

My roomie screamed and quickly scurried out of the room, clearly mortified. I clothed myself and hurried after her in an attempt to remedy the situation. We met in the hall, and I eventually convinced her to come back into the room. I proceeded to explain to her how difficult it had been for me to come out. I didn't know how or when to tell her. She looked understanding, and to my surprise, the situation resolved itself relatively well despite the terrible discomfort. My roomie opted to no longer join her choir group on account of her late departure, and Carrie and I remained on our best behavior for the rest of the weekend.

By Sunday night, Carrie had gone home, and my roomie and I lay in our respective beds in silence. I was sad and uncomfortable, and she was most likely feeling her own set of challenging emotions.

"Lauren?" she called out to me from the darkness.

"Yes?" I responded.

She paused apprehensively. "I don't have to worry about you raping me or anything when you come back drunk, right?"

WHAT? I couldn't muster up any other reaction except laughter. "What do you mean?" I chuckled back, pressed to understand.

My roomie went on to explain that she had heard how people reacted to drinking alcohol (her high school years had been vastly different from mine), and with the recent news about my identity, she was concerned.

I assured her that she had nothing to worry about. There would be no raping, regardless of my alcohol intake or attraction to women.

The rest of my freshman year played out in the same occasionally awkward, comical way. Carrie visited often, and we both shared an eager anticipation for the upcoming year. Carrie was set to attend the city college in Santa Barbara while I jumped full force into my sophomore year. We signed a year lease on an apartment with three close friends, us in one room and the three of them in the other. It would be cramped, but anything was better than constantly freaking out my sheltered roommate. The new roommates definitely knew Carrie and I were an item, and they loved us for it. There was also no risk of them walking in on us. Any inkling of day-to-day comfort in my home would be a welcomed change of pace.

CHAPTER 2

The LA Therapist

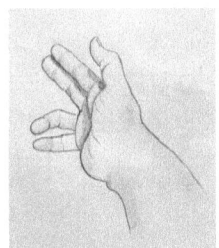

Following an eventful sophomore year filled with constant partying and occasional studying, Carrie and I moved into separate places. Our relationship had begun to lose its magic, and after a two-week breakup, we considered that living apart might allow me the space to address my overwhelming feeling of discontent. Something felt off, and I couldn't quite put my finger on why. My inconsistent emotional state became antithetical to the happiness our relationship once garnered.

Our intimate life dissolved from ecstasy to a sense of complete dissatisfaction on my end in a little less than a year. I no longer liked the way Carrie touched me or how my body felt in response. I grew increasingly self-conscious when naked, and I constantly felt like something was missing. *A penis?* Sex began to feel like a constant loop of foreplay, with no semblance of an obtainable culminating event. My discontent was painfully coupled with a deep envy toward the straight couples in our life. They were able to access heterosexual sex with ease while all we had was a silicone prosthetic, an agonizing replacement of a part I didn't have yet so desperately longed for. I was angered by the drastic shift in my sex life, and deep down, I knew there was nothing I could do. This was surely the painful beginning of something much larger.

Carrie and I were both exasperated by the disconnect, and our interactions with the outside world only served to exacerbate my inability to salvage any part of our once beautiful relationship. The more time we spent out in public, the more uncomfortable I became. I hated the attention our unconventional partnership drew, constantly siphoning away any ability we had to enjoy our time together in peace. Everywhere we went, people would watch Carrie and me, following us with curious eyes while they pondered how our relationship worked. *One of them must be the "man," right?* I was desperate for a reprieve, but the disastrous discontent kept rolling on, growing greater with each passing month.

On our anniversaries, I would cringe as the waiter brought out our celebratory dessert. The candle brought far too much attention, and all eyes in the place would inevitably follow the flame straight to us. *I wonder who the happy couple is?* inquisitive strangers must have thought. I couldn't possibly enjoy the dessert by that point. The discomfort swirling around my insides was impossible to ignore. After dinner, if we went to a party with friends, men would ask us to kiss so they could watch. I despised being some kind of spectacle, standing there together under our very own unwanted spotlight. I wanted to punch all of them, yet somehow disappear at the same time. The tornado of discontent was brewing daily, growing larger and more aggressive with each awful interaction. Something had to give.

Carrie and I broke up right before my senior year, and I ventured off into the world, alone again. She and I simply could not go on with the way things were. She couldn't fix me, and I was honestly unsure of what there was to fix. I sought out employment at the LGBTQ+ resource center on campus in an attempt to find connection or reprieve. I told everyone I was gay, as I hated the word "lesbian" for a reason I didn't yet understand. I had abandoned the bisexual identity in high school, although after Carrie departed, I consistently pursued one man a year to confirm that I was, indeed, still only attracted to women. It wasn't an entirely deliberate quota; there just tended to be about twelve months between my perceived attraction to one man and my pursuit of the next.

I prefaced each intimate interaction with the warning, "I don't like men, so I may not be able to do anything in return." They would often smile, clearly hoping that I was joking, only to find themselves pulling up their pants over an unattended "situation" thirty minutes later. Not a single one of these interactions ever felt right, and I never came remotely close to actually partaking in heterosexual sex. Most of the time, I couldn't get past my jealousy that they were a man with a woman. Talk about a confusing out-of-body experience. It would be years before I realized it was admiration, not attraction, I was feeling.

Outside the random attempts at male connection, my job at the resource center quickly exposed me to a welcoming queer community that I couldn't get enough of. Carrie and I had mostly inhabited straight spaces during our relationship, and suddenly I was without her, surrounded by people that looked like me. There were no more straight, cisgender dudes asking me to kiss other women, and I no longer stood out in the way I despised. The much-needed break from my previous state of constant distress allowed me to embrace who I truly wanted to be for the first time. I began to experiment with my masculinity in response. I cut my hair shorter, finally going above the ears, and gradually changed my entire wardrobe. I still didn't have a penis, but at least I could move away from clothes that accentuated how "female" I was.

With each change I made, the more desirable my aesthetic became to the women in my life. The new attention was nothing short of intoxicating. I suddenly had charged relationships with almost every woman I came across, straight or not, some even ten or more years older than me. My new gauge of self-worth became entirely dependent on this desirability I had fallen into, my day to day serving as a sufficient counter to my increasing discomfort with my body. It didn't matter that I hated my curves more with each passing month. Women loved my feminine features, cloaked in masculinity, and that was all that mattered.

I did all I could to push away the persistent dysphoria for the better part of a year before the tides finally turned. The attention from women was eventually no longer enough, and despite my valiant effort to embody masculinity, I was still frustratingly unable to change any of the overtly feminine parts of me. My curves were only barely concealed under a thin layer of clothing, and I felt sick looking at my reflection on the worst days. Intimacy did nothing to fix it, and painfully, often made it worse. I hated having to constantly acknowledge my breasts and vagina while longing for a flat chest and a penis I would never have. Something was drastically wrong, and the endless stream of disconnected interactions sent me free falling into a deep pit of pain. I felt trapped in my limited ability to present to the world in the way I truly wanted. My breasts pulled at the middle of my button-up shirts, and my hips destroyed any possibility of finding pants I liked. Nothing felt right on me, and I hated myself for it.

In addition to facing the mismatched body I saw in the mirror each morning, menstruating each month made me more miserable than I ever thought possible. I began to toy with the idea that maybe I wasn't just gay. This was more than just being a woman attracted to women. *Maybe there was some type of mistake after my conception? A crossing of paths at some point in utero that caused my brain and body to misalign with one another?* There had to be an explanation. Other lesbians didn't seem to hate their bodies like I hated mine. They were also not overtly concerned with identifying as "lesbian." I was *broken*, and I needed answers. I took a week off school and retreated back to my parents' home for support.

I sat with my mom on our patio the afternoon after I arrived, tears welling in my eyes. The sun burned my forearm as I stared down at it, one of the only parts of my body I actually liked. I couldn't understand why I hated everything else so much. *Other people can't possibly feel this way.* Seemingly out of the blue, my mom said, "When I was pregnant with you, I was convinced I was having a boy. While Dad and I were at the hospital, the Australian National Registry came by, and that's what I told them when they asked." I looked up at her in disbelief. I had one brief moment of peace before I felt like my mind was going to spontaneously combust. It all finally made sense. *My gender has been wrong all along. Even my mom knew it.* "When you were born, we only had a boy's name [James] picked out for you," my mom continued. She and my dad had spent more than a week after I was born deliberating on a girl's name. My birth certificate wasn't finalized with the name Lauren Danielle until September 7th, and I was born on August 27th. I couldn't believe it. I had finally found the smoking gun. *Something did go wrong.*

After arriving back in Santa Barbara following the emotionally turbulent trip home, I was desperate for answers. I sought out one of the counselors at the resource center for help. We met the next afternoon and holed up in her glass-walled office for an hour while I poured my heart out. I was thankful for the opaque panels that ran down the middle of each large window, blocking others in the center from seeing my incessant tears. "Do you know anyone else whose mother sensed their gender was wrong?" I asked her through my blurry eyes. "Do you think I released hormones during utero that made my mom think I was a boy, or did she somehow influence the development of my once female brain by thinking I was?" I pressed on, sucking in air between sentences. I had once read that scientists hypothesized that during development, a signal is sent to the brain at the same time one is sent to the genitals. Typically, the signals align (female-female), but in the case of transgender people, they don't (female-male, in my case).

The counselor stared back at me, clearly in over her head. "I've never met anyone who has said that, but I do know we have lots of literature here in the center that might prove useful," she responded with uncertainty. We spoke long enough for me to calm down, my tear ducts eventually retiring for the day. She slowly unlatched the door, looked over at me encouragingly, and led me over to the plethora of books available for checkout. She picked out a few she felt would be relevant and handed them to me. "Thank you," I said shakily, hoping that I'd find an answer laid out neatly on one of the pages.

I arrived home ten minutes later, grateful that the pile of books stacked on my handlebars hadn't thrown me off balance during my bike ride. I made my favorite snack—a chickenless patty sandwich with sharp cheddar and marinara sauce—and got to work on my literature review. I hadn't even finished the rogue shreds of cheese scattered on my plate before I gave up. I looked at myself in the mirror. "This isn't healthy, is it?" I asked my reflection, consumed by my thoughts. *The further you go down this road in search of an answer, the more likely it is that you will permanently conclude that something is "wrong" with you.* My eyes welled with tears. I knew that wasn't a good mental place to start tackling whatever the monstrous disconnect was. Something had to change, but that didn't mean whatever happened was a mistake. I grew exhausted with the lack of answers, falling asleep that night in a sea of unread pages.

I returned the books the next day, and also reached out to Carter, a transgender man I had recently met through a mutual friend. He and I didn't have much in common, but I was desperately hopeful we'd connect on our gender issues regardless. He was about four years older, sober, and a few months into his transition to male. He wasn't "passing" yet, but it was clear that he had crossed beyond the threshold of masculine woman. I longed to clearly cross that threshold as well, and although we hadn't formed much of a friendship since meeting, I naively assumed he felt all the ways about his gender that I felt about mine, sans having to unpack the information my mom shared. That parental confession seemed pretty damn unique.

I biked down to the local coffee shop, locked up my bike, and made my way through the sea of chairs and tables to join him. Carter had found a private spot in the back with two oversized armchairs, one for him and one for me. I hugged him awkwardly before sitting down, apologizing self-consciously about being all sweaty from cycling. It was now time for our life-changing chat. I studied his body as he spoke, wondering if mine would change in the same way if I took hormones. He was overall thicker than he had been as a woman, and his hair had spread more vastly on his forearms since we'd last seen each other. His voice was slow to catch up, and although he seemed painfully uncertain of himself, he was surely moving toward his peace. I could tell by the glint in his eyes when he smiled. Something made more sense for him now than it did before.

I felt initially calmed by Carter's presence. In our past interactions, I had gotten the impression that he didn't much like me, but this time, his demeanor was clearly more welcoming. After all, he had the upper hand. I was there for his help, and I needed him. I set out to explain to him how I was feeling, desperately hopeful he would relate. I spoke of my poor relationship with my body and how much I hated my curves. I explained how I despised the ways my clothes fit me, the fullness of my thighs and chest. I touched on how I couldn't stand how my breasts hung down during sex and how I wanted to die each time I caught my reflection in the mirror when I was wearing my prosthetic. I studied Carter's face as I explained the hell I was in, and I quickly began to feel disheartened by the lack of acknowledgement from him. He sat there, mostly rigid, sort of inspecting me without offering any form of verbal validation. *Why isn't he at least nodding in agreement with anything I say?*

With each topic I brought up, it became increasingly clear that our gender identities were just an extension of our general lack of connection. We didn't relate on *anything*, and I knew then that I had made a colossal mistake. My body temperature began to spike. I suddenly regretted getting a warm drink.

Following my explanation of how I pictured having a penis during sex, Carter's body language shifted in a way that signaled it was time to end the conversation. "Oh, no. I don't do that," he said as he looked back at me, perplexed. Silence followed, and I couldn't remember the last time I had felt so uncomfortable around another human being. I quickly berated myself for not being prepared for anything other than a "ME TOO!" response from him. I was so eager to hear someone relate to what I was going through, I had blinded myself from the possibility that we might not feel similarly about much at all.

We painfully trudged through a few more topics before I concluded our horrendous coffee date. I never got a true sense of how Carter actually felt, but it was clear that he and I were nothing alike. I left feeling more alone than ever. *If I'm not like Carter, maybe I'm not transgender?* It was a long, lonely ride home, my isolated thoughts cycling more aggressively than the pedals on my bike. I began to worry that there was no one else like me out there. I was lost and confused, unsure of how to proceed. I momentarily wished that I had kept the books. When I got home, I collapsed onto my shaggy brown carpet, defeated and alone. I laid there, staring up at the popcorn ceiling for what felt like an eternity before it hit me. Surely the internet would have some answers. I cautiously typed the query into Google, *I'm a girl that feels like I should be a boy,* and hit ENTER.

A few days later, I sent an email to a fancy psychotherapist in LA whom I had found through my internet search. I had spent hours reading through blogs and Reddit threads the night of my disastrous coffee date, and the majority of the feedback was centered around one thing: talk to a therapist. I followed the suggestion, hopeful that the doctor I had found could help me unpack the disaster unfolding in my head better than Carter did.

Hello, My name is Lauren and I'm a 23-year-old living and working in Santa Barbara, CA. I have come to a point in my life where I feel I need to seek some serious help for my gender & identity issues. I have been out since I was 15 as a lesbian, but the last year has been entirely confusing and difficult trying to process my feelings regarding my desire to be male. Usually about once a month (before menstruation) it gets really difficult, and I feel like an emotional wreck. I feel that this has something to do with an influx of hormones because it is literally like clockwork. I have seen a counselor before at our local LGBTQ center, but I don't feel she was experienced enough in this area to offer me much help.

I am generally a very happy, confident person but cannot seem to figure out if I'm at a point in my life where transitioning will be the only option for me. I feel completely inadequate during some intimate moments and always feel like something is missing. I've tried to find happiness in partners who are supportive and "love me for who I am," but unfortunately that just won't cut it anymore. I need to figure out if there is some way to stop this change in my hormones or maybe if transitioning will ultimately be for me. I've steered clear of the idea because I am terrified of destroying my quality of life during these crucial years of my life.

    I am willing to come down to Los Angeles to see a counselor because I can't do this anymore without help. Your staff sounds wonderfully educated and resourceful, and I would love to speak to someone who has helped many more like myself.

I was relieved when the doctor's response was both encouraging and informative. I set my appointment for 2 pm on September 15, 2012, and watched the calendar like a hawk until the day came. The afternoon of the big meet, I sat anxiously in her foyer unsure of what to expect. *Am I actually transgender? Have other clients felt this exact same way, and that's what brought them here, too?* As the doctor opened her door and ushered me into her office, I felt immediately calmed by her presence. She was both warm and inviting, and I appreciated the lines that formed around her eyes when she smiled. She had lived, and she would surely have some sound advice to offer. "Tell me how you have been feeling. Start from the beginning," she said reassuringly as we took our seats in her huge satin green armchairs. I took a deep breath inward and let loose.

    I pointed out all of the parts of my body I hated, and described in painful detail how disgusted I felt looking in the mirror more days than not. I spoke of how I had learned to close my eyes tightly during sex and picture my body differently to enjoy certain sensations. I shared my newly formed hypothesis as to why I was so vehemently opposed to people referring to me as a lesbian. That word meant I was a woman who liked women, and there was a part of that I didn't agree with. I simply did not feel female. While I explained all the thoughts that had plagued my mind for years, reiterating my entire email in elaborate detail, the doctor barely said a word. She just sat there, staring at me intently. I began to worry, sweat forming aggressively on my temples. *Do I sound crazy? Is this all new to her after all?* I finally stopped talking, took another deep breath, and stared back at her. This was the moment of truth. *Am I unable to be helped? Did I sit in LA rush hour traffic for nothing?*

The doctor looked back at me with that same comforting smile she'd greeted me with in her doorway. "You know," she said, "you don't necessarily have to concretely align with one or the other, male or female."

I looked back at her, perplexed. *What does she know that I don't?*

"Gender is a spectrum, and there are many people that identify as bigender, somewhere between male and female. It's 2012, and we are in a new day and age."

I uncrossed my arms, slightly relaxing the tight grip I had been holding through my muscles. "I hadn't ever considered that," I responded timidly.

She continued on, "You could try living as a combination of both, and if that still doesn't feel right, then you can consider hormones."

I sank back into my chair, suddenly feeling more comfortable with everything around me. A slight tingle of warmth ran up my legs. "I never knew that was a possibility," I said, forming my first smile of the entire session.

We spent the remainder of our time together discussing my options. It was okay if I didn't want to abide by the strict binary expectations of male or female. I could dress as I wanted, and even go as far as telling people I identified as bigender if that felt right for me. I wasn't broken, I was just a teensy bit different than the norm. I had never in my life felt more relieved.

After a long and emotional hug with the doctor, I left the appointment in an absolutely joyous state. I ran down the stairs, out onto the street, and sobbed as I relayed the good news to my parents on the busy sidewalk next to the office building. Concerned strangers curiously peered at me, but for once, I didn't care what anybody else thought. Something had given way inside me, and for the first time in as long as I could remember, I felt free. I had plenty of time and a multitude of options. I wasn't destined to be a lesbian or a woman for the rest of my life—I could live in the grey. I jammed the receipt from the appointment in my wallet and kept it there for three years as a reminder of the momentous occasion. I never saw the therapist again, as I was convinced I didn't need to. I had finally figured everything out. *Life would be smooth sailing from here.*

A few months later, I sat sweating in a chair of a local tattoo shop as the gun pierced black ink permanently into my skin. A grey print out of a bigender symbol sat on the shiny metal tray next to me. I had impulsively decided to rubber stamp my bigender identity, the new tattoo serving as a reminder that I could live in the middle, just like the doctor had suggested. I didn't have to hate myself for not being biologically male, and it was okay that I didn't quite fit as female. I had found my peace in the grey, and things were looking up.

Living in the grey

CHAPTER 3

Blue Island in a Sea of Red

After graduating from college, I stayed in Santa Barbara and worked six nights a week at the Beachside Bar Cafe, a restaurant on the beach that I mostly loved. I had worked there since just before my senior year and made a good amount of cash. I was also surrounded by gorgeous "straight" women who seemed to have an affinity for my quasi-masculine presentation. I was constantly in and out of a relationship with one of the hostesses and lived in a rowdy house downtown with three guys from the wait staff. It was a hot, incestuous mess, and I reveled in the much-needed break after finishing school.

There was only one downside to the young adult playground I inhabited—the predominantly male management team that ran it. I was one of many twenty-something-year-olds running around in short khaki shorts, a Hawaiian shirt, and long white socks with running shoes. The outfit was both playfully cute and a recipe for disaster. I was slightly more masculine than the other women, especially equipped with my newfound bigender identity, but it didn't matter. The men didn't discriminate—a nice ass was a nice ass. As a "female" looking person in this environment, one quickly understands that a little sexual harassment must be tolerated in order to remain gainfully employed. I had already learned this lesson a few years prior.

During a slow afternoon at my freshmen college job at Chili's, I was helping a male manager apply "$2.99" stickers to our menus. I had always liked him. He spoke fondly of his daughter and reminded me of my own dad, who is my favorite person. While he and I were chatting back and forth, he pulled a sticker off the sheet and shot me a playful smile. He suddenly extended out his arm and placed the bright red sticker on my left breast, followed by a tasteless comment about me also costing $2.99. The safe, fatherly façade fell away in an instant. He was nothing like my dad after all. I was furious. I quickly peeled the sticker off my breast and playfully told him to stop it, in an attempt to conceal my anger. My body was hot with rage, but I knew that I was powerless. This type of "harmless" interaction was just part of life as a woman.

Beachside continued with the same unfortunate, yet predictable narrative. Every time I entered the kitchen to grab the ice cream base for a chocolate sundae, all the cooks would turn to gawk at my thighs and ass. They would make comments and snicker among themselves. I could either disapprovingly scowl at them or flash a flirty smile. I wanted my customers' food to be ready on time, so I'd flash the smile instead of the scowl.

They would smile back, and all would be right in the world for a brief moment. After the sundaes, I'd head to the bar to pick up my drinks. Every time without fail, it was essential that I flirt with the male bartenders while they made my drinks. If I ignored their remarks, they would choose to make my drinks last. If I played along, my drinks would be made in a timely manner. I needed my drinks to be on time to ensure a good tip from the thirsty customers, so I begrudgingly played along.

The feeling of being reduced to a sexual object was not a good one, although I slowly came to terms with it. Whether in the restaurant or out in the world, men could do as they pleased and women simply had to put up with it. *Understood*. I had grown up with a dad free from the poison of toxic masculinity, but the majority of men I encountered appeared to be different. This would make for a confusing juxtaposition when I eventually shifted to "manhood" myself. For now though, all I really had to worry about was my parents' incessant nagging. They would not stop bugging me about using the college degree they had just paid for. *Privilege alert*. It was time for me to get a job that was actually relevant to my studies.

I sent out resumes for a couple months before I finally got a hit. I was awoken one Monday morning after a night out at our local gay bar, Wildcat, to an official-sounding woman asking me about my application. I had no idea what she was talking about, but played along as if I did. Two days later, I was scheduled to meet the hiring manager at a local medical device company. The interview was nerve-racking, and I worked diligently to convince myself that wearing a suit as a woman was acceptable.

If they don't want to hire you on account of your appearance, you don't want to work for them, I told myself. My intuition was correct, and I jumped in feet first once I landed the job, suits and all. I loved the work—capturing complaint information while helping women with their breast implant warranties. It was interesting and challenging, and somewhat overlapped with my prior experience in healthcare. I wasn't going to med school like I had initially planned, but I could still use what I had learned from my courses and endless hospital volunteer hours to facilitate my success.

Four months into my promising new role, the company informed us that they were shutting down the Santa Barbara site. The staff were given the option of being laid off or relocating to Austin, Texas. Considering I was only twenty-three and stuck in a toxic on-and-off relationship with the restaurant hostess, I chose the latter. I had nothing to lose and was an ambitious little muffin, ready to catapult my career forward. I convinced the company to make me permanent and cover the majority of my relocation costs. Luckily for me, not many people were willing to leave liberal, sunny Santa Barbara for the hot, conservative Texas landscape.

A few months later, equipped with my new employee ID, I broke up with my girlfriend for the fourteenth and final time and set out on the twenty-hour road trip from California to Texas with my dad. A few hours in, I was consumed with worry as I stared out the car window into the nothingness. Miles and miles of desert, broken up only by sleepy little towns sprinkled along a seemingly never-ending stretch of highway. I wished for any inkling of a distraction; my dad and I had mostly run out of things to say by the time we'd hit Arizona. Sitting in silence, I obsessed over how my identity and overall aesthetic would be received in the Longhorn state. Most of my friends in Santa Barbara had met me with a "YOU are moving to Texas??" when I announced the big move. Their concern, although not unwarranted, only served to exacerbate my fears. All we knew of Texas was bigots, guns, and overtly religious folks. *Quite disconcerting, I must admit.* "Don't worry, Austin is supposedly a blue island in the sea of red," I'd often respond, running my hand over the slight raise of my bigender tattoo. "I'll be fine," I told them, trying to muster up any sense of conviction.

During an overnight stay in lovely El Paso, I messaged an old acquaintance whom I had worked with at the Chili's in Santa Barbara and who had since also moved to Austin. I figured securing at least one point of connection prior to my arrival would help quell my nerves. I was desperate to avoid the impending isolation I knew would come. Stacey wasn't queer, but I had always felt comfortable around her. She could care less that I liked women and there had never been any tension between us. *Rare.* I was relieved when my phone pinged and the little blue response bubble popped up. Stacey expressed excitement to reconnect and even offered to introduce me to the queer circle of friends she occasionally socialized with. She had recently been brought into the group by a coworker of hers. My eyes lit up when I saw the words. I couldn't wait to meet them.

Days later, my dad was off to the airport and I was left alone in a dark Austin hotel room unable to fall back asleep. I had awoken when he kissed me goodbye at 5am and my nerves had refused to let up since. *What would I wear? What would my new coworkers think of me?* Only two other people from the Santa Barbara site had relocated. Everyone else would be new, although I had quasi met some of them through the company's instant messenger application. My coworkers were supposedly excited to meet me, but my cruel mind convinced me that would change in person regardless. After two hours of watching the sun slowly creep in through the thick, heavy curtains, it was time. I showered, went to the bathroom at least three times, and headed out the door in the most neutral outfit I could muster. I parked my car in the lot and anxiously wondered if my new coworkers were watching me through the windows as I approached the building. "Lauren looks different in person than I imagined," they would most certainly say to one another. My chest grew tight and more uncomfortable with each step I took.

Within minutes of meeting the six new members of the team, I was able to relax a smidge. They were friendly and inviting, and no one seemed put off by my masculine presentation. One of my new coworkers, Jamie, was a gay man and it was only a matter of days before we started enjoying the pleasures of after-work happy hours together. I was relieved by his presence. He was intelligent, quippy as hell, and we were both part of the community I loved so dearly. The next few weeks were a blur of meeting the rest of the office, finding an apartment, and trying all of the breakfast taco spots within a ten-mile radius that Jamie recommended. *Taco Deli, you are #1.*

On the weekends, Jamie and I spent ample time together, him eventually accompanying me to Houston to fulfill a lifelong dream of mine: getting a corgi. I had been obsessed with corgis for many years, and once I got settled in Austin, I figured it was a good time to get one. I was in a new place with a new life, and was a tad lonely when I wasn't hanging out with Jamie and his adorable pug, Gizmo. I was eager for companionship, especially after seeing those two together. I found a family in Houston via Petfinder that had a fifteen-month-old corgi that needed rehoming. She was tan and white, and absolutely gorgeous. I reached out to the owner immediately.

The following weekend, Jamie and I made the three-hour trip in his car. We talked of our pasts, our identities, and our desires for the future. I was thankful for the time to get to know one another. Once we arrived in Houston, we followed the GPS to a small town on the outskirts of the city. We eventually found the house, and Jamie parked across the street, avoiding the many children running around outside. We slowly exited the car and approached the front door. I knocked nervously, and a stressed-out mom answered. Within seconds, Danica, their corgi, came running up to my feet and sat down, all the while looking directly into my eyes. The owner looked shocked. "She's never done that with anyone," she exclaimed. I smiled down at the little ball of fluff, eager to make her mine. I stepped inside with Jamie, nervous that we would soon come face to face with her large, gun-toting Texan husband I'd made up in my head.

There was no husband, but the house was awful. Dark

and dingy, with an entire wall in the living room covered in crosses from top to bottom. I'm surprised we didn't burst into flames right then and there. Danica followed us around, clearly as desperate as we were to get out of there. There were crates everywhere, dogs barking incessantly from random rooms, and the children from the street were tracking mud all over the carpet while we talked.

"I've just gone back to work and need to get rid of some of my additional responsibilities," the lady said as she looked down at Danica. My initial concern that I'd be denied the adoption based on my appearance quickly diminished. "You can have her for $300," she continued on.

Conveniently, that was all I had left from the relocation package my work had given me. "You've got a deal!" I responded excitedly. I fished the bills out of my pocket, picked up Danica, and we were on our way.

I was beaming from ear to ear as I loaded her into the car. "Let's get the fuck out of here," I said to Jamie as we clicked in our seat belts. As Jamie pulled away, I looked back at my new friend, soon to be renamed Bailee. She was drooling everywhere and she was perfect.

Bailee and I soon established quite the routine, and any loneliness I felt previously quickly disappeared. We would cuddle each morning and miss each other all day until I got home from work. We spent our evenings going on walks, exploring new dog parks, and having dinner with Jamie and Gizmo. I was immediately more at ease once I had a semblance of a routine established. I have always been a sucker for consistency.

Soulmates

As I began to feel more comfortable in Austin, I grew eager to expand my social life. Jamie and I remained close, but I knew it was time to meet the queer group that Stacey had told me so much about. Stacey lived conveniently close to my work, so we agreed to have dinner at her house for our reunion. I fed Bailee and tucked her warmly into her crate before I drove over. Stacey had a cat that had never met a dog, and Bailee wasn't an ideal candidate for a first meet. She was quite the bundle of energy.

Stacey and I were fast friends, bonding over the ridiculous male managers at Chili's. We often joked about why we weren't closer in Santa Barbara. We began to hang out frequently, and it wasn't long before she invited me to a house party with her queer friends. I was painfully nervous as we headed over. I hadn't been around a new group of queer people since college, and I fretted that they wouldn't accept me. *Were queer people different in Austin? Would I not fit in for some intangible reason?* My heart was pattering loudly as we parked, but Stacey grabbed my hand and dragged me inside with a smile. I was relieved when the door sprung open, and we were met by her friendly coworker. They hugged us both warmly, Stacey a little tighter as they were already acquainted.

I followed them timidly down the cold, tile walkway out to the vast, lusciously green backyard. As the door slid open, I was met with a large group of people, some standing and some sitting. I introduced myself slowly and deliberately to each of them and took a seat. We spoke of Santa Barbara and what had brought me out to Austin. I told them I was bigender and shared my past struggles with my identity. I was relieved by the welcoming undertones and thrilled to find that there was a transman in the group. Peter was incredibly handsome, confident, and had a strikingly attractive girlfriend, which made me hopeful in a way that I couldn't quite place.

Thanks to Stacey's introduction, my afternoons and weekends were quickly filled to the brim with plans. Bailee and I were both happy with the added attention. The new friend group was a hodgepodge of people, all falling somewhere on the queer spectrum, some close to where I was at the time. We spent our days by any form of water and our nights dancing at the local gay bars. I quickly grew close to Peter, and obsessively focused on all aspects of his life. *Is he happy? Does he like being a man?* I envied the way his clothes fit him and how flat his chest looked, scars and all. It felt right being together, like some form of brotherhood I didn't yet understand. He and others in the group would often ask me if I planned to transition, but after I requested they stop, their caring inquiries quickly ceased. "Maybe she doesn't know it yet?" they would surely say to one another when I left.

The next few months were a whirlwind of attempting to balance work with my budding social life. After I began to date in the group, there were nights I would come home at 6am only to get up forty-five minutes later for work. *Sorry, Bailee.* I was completely consumed by the attention, and it wasn't long before I jeopardized my new friendships on account of whom I pursued romantically. One member of the group quickly grew angry with me after I began to date their roommate, their anger only made worse when the girl they liked took a fancy to me too. I couldn't blame their response, but I was unable to stop myself. The cycle was repeating itself, and I was desperate for distraction like I had been during my days in Santa Barbara. My female identity still wasn't right.

I eventually settled into a longer-term relationship with a woman named Constance, an acquaintance of one of my coworkers. We were madly in love, but behind the scenes of my happy persona, my struggle with the female characteristics of my body continued to destroy me from the inside out. I was powerless over how I felt about my voluptuous breasts and curvy hips no matter how Constance felt about them. To make matters worse, my recently found bigender identity was of no relevance to the straight world. The majority of society perceived me as female, and therefore, that's what I was. A majority of my time spent outside of my relationship and queer social bubble began to horribly resemble the dreaded candle scenario from my anniversaries with Carrie. My overtly masculine presentation continued to confuse mostly anyone who wasn't queer, and I was rarely able to exist unnoticed. Women would freak out when they saw me in the restroom, thinking that a man had somehow read the sign on the door incorrectly. *Really?*

I was deemed the token lesbian in the office and was unable to have a short haircut or wear men's clothing without standing out. On a particularly bad day at work, a female boss even went as far as suggesting I dress more feminine for an internship interview I had scheduled for that weekend. "Maybe you should wear something a little softer. That will make it more likely they will choose you," she suggested. "There's a great sale on blouses right now at Kohl's," she continued on smiling, unaware of how offensive it all was. *How lucky I am to have a boss like her.* I grew distraught at her painfully insensitive suggestion and left work immediately following our conversation. I could barely see the road through my tears as I drove home. Bailee snuggled me extra close that night. She has always known when I'm not okay.

The constant anxiety and discomfort grew to be crippling, interfering dramatically with my ability to enjoy my day-to-day. Life was a constant struggle to blend or assimilate, and I mostly wanted to disappear in any setting that wasn't queer. It didn't matter that the salesgirls at work smiled at me or that my girlfriend was already talking about marriage. My worsening dysphoria was spiraling, and I couldn't stand how I was perceived. My menstrual cycle continued to worsen, eventually leading me to consider the idea of suicide. With the influx of estrogen, my breasts would get larger and more tender while my emotional state dipped below its typical baseline. Some months were better than others, but the more time passed, the greater the despair became. I'd sink to the bathroom floor, crying for hours, unable to face the situation any longer.

Coupled nicely with the despair came a horrendous sense of guilt. My life was so perfect, what could I possibly be so unhappy about? Amazing parents, awesome friends, a super-hot girlfriend, and a great job. *What else could a person want?* I felt so incredibly ungrateful, consumed with the belief that this was all just some cruel joke. I could have everything, but my body would always be wrong. The curse of it all. I pictured myself as a flower with glorious sunlight and moist soil, only to be poisoned from within by a toxic water supply—my brain's absolute disdain for my physical being, which continued to worsen with each passing year. *I can't do this forever,* played over and over in my head. I knew something had to change and was scared shitless when suicide began to feel like a viable option. *Maybe I could end this life and come back as something else?*

No matter what, I knew I couldn't leave Earth that way regardless of how bad it got. My parents would never recover, and I owed them more than that. They had always been so wonderful. I wasn't ready to consider the terrifying world of hormones, but I still had options. I desperately wanted to change everything "female" about my body, my breasts being the overwhelming focal point. I turned to Google for the second most important search in my journey: *top surgery doctors in Texas*. I hoped that removing my breasts would somehow be enough to combat my daily dysphoria. I would only entertain the idea of hormones if it wasn't.

CHAPTER 4

Departure of the Arch Nemeses

After much research and hours spent scrolling through images of peoples' chests, I contacted the office of a renowned top surgery doctor in Plano, Texas. The staff were friendly and informative, and we ultimately decided on April 29, 2015, for my surgery date. I had a work trip in March, so we had to wait until the following month. In the meantime, I had a few to-dos: contact my insurance company, coordinate my time off work, and go to therapy. The first two were relatively painless, albeit still daunting.

As expected, contacting my insurance provider was awkward and ridiculous. They could not understand why I wanted my breasts cut off and refused to acknowledge that gender dysphoria fell into the "medically necessary" category. *Considering suicide seems pretty damn dire to me.* I failed to convince them otherwise, so resorted to taking out a no-interest credit card instead. I wouldn't be able to pay it off before the interest hit, but selfishly knew my parents would be there regardless. A privilege most LGBTQ+ folks do not have.

After requesting PTO from work for an undisclosed surgery, I begrudgingly set out to find a therapist. I was angered by the notion that I couldn't be trusted to make this decision myself. I had hated my breasts for years and felt a stranger didn't need to approve that I knew what I was doing to my body. To add insult to injury, therapists in the area were charging over $120 an hour, and the insurance company refused to assist once again. I didn't have the money or the desire, but I had no other choice. My doctor required six months of weekly therapy prior to the procedure. It didn't matter that I wasn't on hormones; the rules were the rules. I was destined to spend almost twenty-four hours of my life in the near future talking solely about my breasts. *Damn it.*

I found a transgender therapist near my work and lasted three sessions before I begged her to let me switch to biweekly. Her office was dark, dingy, and had an inordinate amount of woodwork. Whether it was the horrible vibe of the space, the "get on with it" approach I'd been raised with, or my own guilt complex, the end of our fifty minutes couldn't come soon enough. No matter how the therapist acted or what she said, I was convinced that she was judging me. *Look at this spoiled little shit*, she probably thought. *No trauma, Mommy and Daddy to pay for everything, just in case. She doesn't know how good she has it.* To this day, my chest still tightens when I think about it.

Two months into the required six, I called the doctor's office to convince them I could be done with therapy. I stood in the dairy aisle at HEB, a local grocery store, staring at cheeses while I pitched my case to his office manager. I hoped the people around me weren't listening too intently. "Is there any way the doctor will do the surgery with only three months of therapy? I literally don't know what to talk about with this therapist." I was met with silence on the other end of the line. "I know I want to get my boobs off. I've hated them since the moment they came in. What else do you need?" The office manager assured me she understood my angst, although I doubted she truly did. "Let me call you back after I speak to the doctor." I thanked her, grabbed a salad, and headed back to work hopeful that the doctor would approve my request.

The office manager called the next day and relayed the good news. My wish would be granted. The doctor approved the reduction in therapy, and I strategically avoided telling them I had only been going every other week. I couldn't wait for it to be over. *One step closer to freedom.* The only hurdle that remained was a work trip to the Philippines. I had been selected to train a group of individuals at our remote site in Cebu for two weeks. I was ecstatic for the professional opportunity, yet completely overtaken with fear for how my gender expression would surely be perceived in this foreign place. The impending discomfort was almost too much to bear, and to make matters worse, I would be joining an old coworker and manager from Santa Barbara who hadn't seen me in years. They would be shocked by the change in my external presentation, and I obsessed over what they would think. *What happened to her? She used to be so pretty.* I desperately tried to convince myself it would be okay, but the moment I stepped off the plane, my concerns were quickly validated. The two-week jaunt in the Philippines turned out to be my last emotional tailspin of a hurrah before I drastically changed the trajectory of my life for good.

From the moment I stepped off the plane, I was constantly called "sir" in front of both of my coworkers. The straight, conservative male manager did a decent job hiding his discomfort, but each time it happened, my chest wound tight and I grew increasingly more nauseated as the seconds passed. I looked for comfort from my female coworker, but she either didn't see me or wasn't interested in helping. When we arrived at the office, the situation somehow grew more dire. I was introduced to a room full of strangers failing to hide their confusion—almost twenty pairs of eyes trying to understand my short haircut, masculine clothing, and contrasting female curves. My presentation was so mixed at that point, it was clear they didn't know what to make of me. Apparently, they had never seen a masculine-presenting woman before. I held my breath each time I walked into the women's restroom, hoping that no one else was in there. I was rarely so lucky.

I did all I could to focus on my work, but with each passing day, I failed worse than the last. Halfway through the first of two weeks, I couldn't take it anymore. I blamed my unspecified physical ailments on jetlag and requested to be taken back to the hotel by our driver. It was the best excuse I could muster up without jeopardizing my career. Either way, I didn't care anymore. I needed any excuse to be alone in my hotel room, away from the world that made me so uncomfortable I wanted to die. I spent the remainder of that day crying, speaking to Constance and my parents on Skype, and sitting on the toilet trying to poop. I had been constipated for days on end on account of the stress. The physical discomfort was unbearable by the fourth day. *How has my life come to this?*

Hotel refuge

I hoped the weekend would be better. The manager had separate plans, and my female coworker and I had a weekend of island hopping and whale shark–swimming ahead of us. I tried to make way for a little excitement. Surely being away from the stress caused by the confused staff and undesirable bathroom encounters would help. *Wrong.* Everywhere we went, the locals stared at me with confusion just like the people in the office had. I tried to convince myself that perhaps I was overthinking it, but deep down I knew that wasn't the case. I was simply unable to ignore their perplexed looks. *Had they never seen a short-haired woman in board shorts and a sports bra before?* Any progress my stomach had made was stopped in its tracks.

As we swam with the whale sharks off the coast, instead of focusing on the beautiful twenty-ton animals only five feet away, all I could think about was how much I despised my body. I couldn't stand how my breasts looked in my sports bra top or how my hips pulled my board shorts tight in all the wrong ways. My thighs somehow looked even bigger underwater, and the way my stomach spilled over the side edges of the waistband was utterly disgusting. I hated myself for letting this once-in-a-lifetime experience be spoiled by my dysphoria. I so desperately wanted to enjoy these precious moments. Years later, I still feel ashamed when the whale shark image pulls up on the scroll of Apple TV away images.

The trip never improved. I got sick twice and my stomach situation never truly gave way. I was relieved when the second week of our training finally ended. I only had to hide my feelings from my female coworker for a few more hours as we departed for the airport; the manager was scheduled to stay another week. I envied how simple this must all be for him. Just walking around as a straight, white man in a body that made sense. *I'm sure he doesn't have to even think about using the restroom.* I pushed down my emotions as they boiled up inside me, ready to spill over. *Almost there, Lauren. It'll be over soon.* After we got through customs and left for our separate gates, I sat by myself, stewing on my self-disdain. I was trapped and had never felt so much pain in my life. We finally boarded, and the moment I plopped down in my seat, I cried so hard I worried I might throw up right then and there. All the years of distress suddenly culminated in that moment. I had never wanted anything to end more in my life, and I could barely bring myself to care that other people had noticed my incessant tears. The situation couldn't possibly get worse. After three connecting flights, I finally made it home to Constance and Bailee for snuggles. I couldn't wait to start pulling myself out of this fucking nightmare.

A week later, I stood in my living room as my roommate held the camera steady. The top half of my body was fully exposed, my tubular breasts pointing downward at the angle that I hated more than anything else about them. The doctor had requested that I email him pictures from all sides. He had to know what he was working with and whether or not I would need liposuction under my arms. Standing there topless, I was embarrassed and ashamed even though I knew my housemates understood. I had moved into a house with Jamie, another coworker Matt, and Constance almost a year prior. The three of them had been front and center to my ongoing distress. On the night we met, I told Constance, "I'm getting my boobs cut off next year." *At least she knew what she was getting herself into?* After we moved in together, she eventually gave up half our shared wardrobe to my blazer collection, a futile attempt to conceal my breasts. Texas summers were no fun.

April 29th quickly approached, accompanied by an all-too-familiar looming sense of guilt. Not only did I have everything, I was now cutting into a perfectly healthy body for a reason that many probably wouldn't understand. I hated that this was my only option, and I desperately wanted to fast forward through the next few months. There had to be something better on the other side of this. That's what all the "It Gets Better" commercials had promised. The day of my pre-op appointment, I glanced around nervously as I got seated in the doctor's waiting room. *Were there other people like me here?* The doctor's staff called my name, and Constance and I proceeded into the examination room.

We sat there jovially taking selfies, sharing in the excitement of the moment. The doctor came in full of enthusiasm and shook my hand with force. I felt a familiar sense of envy as I surveyed his muscular frame and dark features. He was handsome and had naturally been born with the beautifully contoured chest he possessed. "Hey, man!" he exclaimed, distracting me from my staring. *Nice validation, doc.* I slipped the robe down to my waist per his request and stood there while he poked and prodded. I did all I could to push away the feelings of shame as the doctor squeezed each breast to establish fat content. He punched his hand into my chest as he concluded the examination, "Nice chest, man!" I appreciated the doctor's genuine efforts to make me feel even a tiny bit less female.

We discussed my expectations, and I showed the doctor some pictures of what I didn't want. A few of the results I'd seen online displayed a continuous scar on the chest that looked like a W, a U around each breast where they had been cut off. I didn't mind the idea of the scars, but I most definitely did not want that. I couldn't give people any reason to suspect my scars were the result of a potential breast removal.

"Are those my results?!" the doctor exclaimed, clearly surprised.

"No, these are results I have seen online," I responded.

"Phew," he said. "Not to worry, man, your scars will look nothing like that."

I was relieved. The doctor appeared confident and sure of himself. Two things I wasn't feeling a whole lot of at the time.

Following the Q&A, I was moved into a cold, barren photography room so his staff could take more photos of my breasts. This photoshoot was significantly more humiliating than the one my roommates and I had held in the privacy of our home. I stared around shamefully while the camera clicked over and over. *I wonder if they think I'm a freak too?* I forced my mind to cease the unhelpful, self-disdaining spiral. These people were medical professionals, and I had nothing to be ashamed of. I was relieved when it ended and Constance and I could head back to the hotel. I wrote a letter to my body that night to help manage my tumultuous emotions.

> To my body,
>
> I have such mixed feelings about our top surgery. I am so excited to have this part of you gone, but I feel such immense guilt for the pain you will feel as a result. When this is over, there will be two giant scars left across your chest where two perfectly healthy breasts used to be. I

love you, but you know I have always hated them. I have tried my best for years to flatten them down and ignore the painful tenderness that would come with each period. This part of you has always caused me so much anxiety. I remember the first time Mom suggested a bra to hold them in. I was ten years old and none of it made sense. I clipped it on to hold them inside. It never felt right. I wanted them free, but they had gotten too big for that. I remember walking back to class from lunch when the clasp came undone. They popped free, and I was mortified. I went to the bathroom and tried to contain them once again into the awkward cloth apparatus.

The discomfort has gone on for too many years. Sports bras are better, but I want there to be nothing. I want our chest to be free like my brother's. It has all become too much to bear. Clothing always looks wrong on you because of them. Nothing can ever hold them flat enough in my button-ups for the shirt button to not pull in the middle. Everything looks too round. It isn't your fault, but I can't take it anymore. I have desperately tried to find exercises that will take the fullness down, but to no avail. They never work, and I feel like leaving all of you behind because of it. No matter what happens tomorrow, I want you to know that I love you so much. Thank you for enduring all this pain for me. I promise you it will be worth it. I know you will look perfect when this is all over.

Love,
Me

The next morning, I laid down on the gurney anxious for what the next few hours would hold. As they wheeled me back to the pre-op area, I worried that I might not wake up from anesthesia. *You wouldn't know either way*, I reassured myself. The doctor came in just as enthusiastically as he had during our first appointment. "You ready?!" he asked jovially. "More ready than I'll ever be," I responded, filled with hope. He uncapped his pen and drew lines across my chest to mark where he would make the incisions. He then drew circles where my new nipples would go. I anxiously overanalyzed the placement of each pen stroke. The permanent marker burned my nostrils as I looked down. I worried incessantly that he had drawn the nipples too far apart, but quickly reminded myself that he was the expert. The doctor paused and looked at me for my approval of the new nipple positioning. "What do you think?" he said excitedly. I quickly nodded in agreement and laid my head down on the starchy pillow. *I can't believe I just okayed how part of my body will be permanently replaced.*

The staff wheeled me off, and the next coherent moment I had is one I will never forget. I sat up ever so slightly in the hospital bed, groggy still from the anesthesia. Constance held my hand and looked caringly into my fuzzy eyes. "How do you feel?" she inquired excitedly. "I feel good," I responded while my lips turned upward and my eyes looked down. I couldn't believe it was finally over. My chest was finally flat, and there were bandages where the two lumps used to be. *I wonder what they did with my breasts. Did they just throw them away?* I momentarily felt a wave of sadness pass through me as I pictured them sitting in a trash bag somewhere.

Immediately after, I was flooded with an unmatched feeling of reassurance. I knew at that moment that I was going to transition. Top surgery wasn't going to cut it after all. *No pun intended*, I laughed to myself. I pushed the fear of hormones out of my mind and momentarily let myself enjoy the recent departure of my arch nemeses. Soon after the anesthesia wore off, Constance and I headed back to the hotel to rest. Everything was sore and tender, but the combination of excitement and painkillers drowned all of that out. After a decent night's sleep, we headed back to Austin. I looked excitedly out the window as we navigated the highways. I knew in my soul I was on the right track, and I was desperate for more of this feeling. I sank into the cushy seat and smiled as the sun's warm rays danced across my face.

I had to wait anxiously for one week before I went back to Plano to see what my chest would look like for the rest of my life. The buildup was excruciating. I trusted the doctor had done well, and I strictly followed all the post-op instructions he had given me. I had to wear bandages for a month and was not allowed to stretch my scars in any way. Each day, Constance would wrap and unwrap the bandages when I wanted to shower. They had to be nice and tight to keep the swelling down. The sensation was strangely reminiscent of wearing a binder to flatten my breasts in the past, and it was odd for the feeling to be garnered from a different, much happier set of circumstances. My roommates were there for emotional support just in case. Before work, they would leave everything by my bedside so I wouldn't have to move much during the day.

When they were gone, Bailee and I would cuddle up and watch Netflix. She would cautiously move herself up the comforter, clearly aware that my chest was a place to stay away from. I had never seen her do anything like it, and it made my recovery a whole lot more tolerable. I honestly can't imagine recovering from a surgery without her.

Seven long days later, my parents finally arrived in Austin to take me to my post-op appointment. It was time to introduce my new nipples to the world, and I could barely contain myself. During my post-op, I sat in the chair anxiously awaiting the removal of the bandages. Each nipple was covered with a square gauze pad that said "DO NOT REMOVE" written in thick, black Sharpie. *They meant business.* My chest was tender along the incision lines and underneath each armpit. Liposuction had left a slew of black and blue bruises down my sides that were hands down the most uncomfortable part of recovery. The nurses took great care as they removed all of the bandaging. As I felt them peel off the last piece of dressing, I looked down to greet my new chest for the first time. The area was still so red and swollen, and the scars looked undeniably grotesque, but behind the evidence of the recent battle proudly stood the chest I had always wanted. *Beautiful.* I felt shivers all over. The staff cleaned me up, provided the necessary aftercare instructions, and we were on our way. I couldn't wait to show the world.

My parents and I celebrated my immediate relief as we navigated the roads of Plano to find the highway back to Austin. For the first time in my life, I had an inkling of comfort in my own skin. Something finally felt right, and there was surely more to come. I had to let my parents in on my desire to pursue hormones. We had four hours left of the drive, and I hoped that would be enough time to answer all of their questions. I paused our momentary celebration and explained the clarity I had felt when I woke up from surgery.

"I want to tell you both something," I said, glancing at their faces as the energy shifted ever so slightly. "When I woke up from surgery, I felt more clarity than I've ever felt. There was a wave of certainty that overtook me when I looked down. I now know I'm transgender, and I can't stop with this surgery." I watched my dad's eyes slip into emptiness. My mom grabbed my hand, rubbing her thumb warmly across the top of it. "I want to wait at least two months until I start hormones, but I'm going to start looking for a doctor now." I had a feeling testosterone (T) would make me feel insane, and I had eight weeks after surgery before I was cleared to restart my exercise routine. I couldn't risk jumping into that terrifying world without ample energy expenditure to offset the intensity.

My mom asked many questions and was welcoming of the news. Considering the recent-ish disclosure regarding her thoughts when she was pregnant with me, I wasn't all that surprised. She had clearly expected this. My dad sat almost silent in the backseat, his mind consumed with worry as he stared blankly off into the distance. I obsessively watched his face in the rearview mirror, looking back to the road every so often to avoid an accident. Unlike my mom, my dad had clearly been in denial that I would ever actually transition.

There had been so many conversations about it those past few years, but that didn't help him feel any more prepared.

"Everything will be so much more complicated," he said, his voice filled with desperation. It wasn't that he didn't want a transgender child, he just wanted my suffering to end. "I want you to be able to get on with your life, and now you won't be able to do that," he expressed. He had been so hopeful that top surgery would be the answer, although Mom and I knew deep down it wouldn't be. I'd clung on to the life raft as long as I could, and now it was time to jump into the rapids. "I know, Dad, but I don't have a choice. I can't spend the rest of my life as a woman, with or without breasts." He was unable to muster up a response. This was the one thing that he couldn't fix, and the resulting pain in his eyes was unbearable to witness. He couldn't make sense of my inner turmoil any more than I could, and I felt so guilty for dragging him through the mud with me. I have never in my life seen someone so strong look so helpless. He didn't want to accept that this was only the beginning of a painful, treacherous journey into the unknown for his little girl.

My parents and I eventually made it back to Austin after much more discussion. "Everything is going to be okay," I told them as they unloaded their luggage at the airport the following morning. "We love you," they said as they wrapped their arms around me, careful to avoid the tender parts.

I went back to work the next day, a tad emotional and hopeful that my button-ups would somehow hide the lumpiness underneath. I hadn't offered an explanation to any of my coworkers in an attempt to avoid their inevitable questions. *They couldn't possibly understand.* When one coworker went in for a big hug to welcome me back, she surprisingly responded, "I know," when I requested she be gentle. Maybe people had figured it out after all. *If I don't bring it up, they can't either.* I pushed on, and after the bandages were gone, my chest was finally free. Feeling the wind pass uninterrupted across my chest still stands as one of the greatest sensations of my lifetime. *Peter, you were right.*

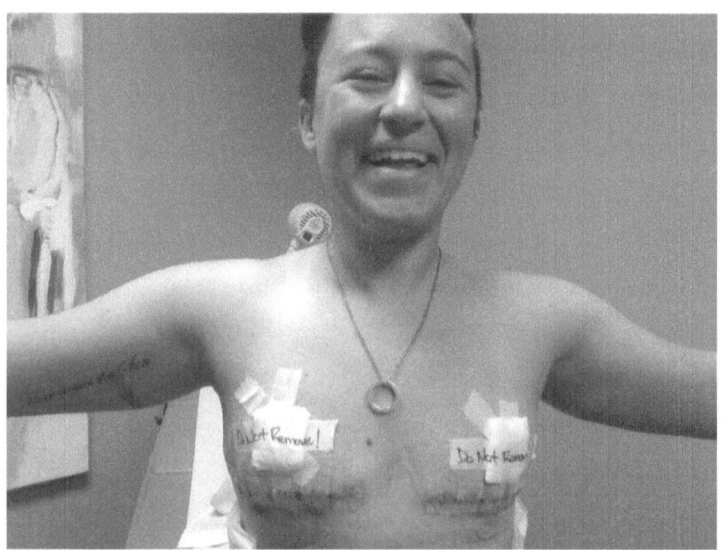

Freedom

HOW DID YOU PERCEIVE MY IDENTITY BEFORE I TRANSITIONED?

"You seemed more comfortable with masculinity, and I definitely picked up on that energy. I think I more so paid attention to your sexual identity journey and didn't realize it was really about gender."

Jill / Friend / California

"I don't remember perceiving anything about your identity. To me, you were a funny queer girl who I enjoyed talking to like one of the guys, just like one of my best friends in high school. You were the first trans person I knew (after you came out), and it was outside the realm of my experience to question my own gender."

Clint / Coworker, Friend / Austin

"I remember you first identified as bisexual, then lesbian, then as bigender, and finally as male. I didn't necessarily question your identity as a female, but seeing you become James made it clear you were male all along."

Kaitlin / Friend / California

"In high school, your gender expression was female, albeit far from femme, and orientation was evolving and developing. Growing up in an area that generally lacked diversity, particularly a queer community, there weren't resources available for those who didn't live in black and white.

You were in a gray area with your gender identity that became colorful when you relocated to Austin, Texas. I believe you were hedging on how to identify because lesbian didn't fit the bill, and straight didn't fit the body."

Rachel / Friend / California

"I knew that you were my friend Lauren, who was a lesbian, so if I did have any concept about your gender identity, it was more of a function—or output—of your sexual orientation: 'Lauren loves women.'

I knew that you hated your breasts, but I never associated that with your larger identity for some reason. It may have been that it was a feature that was so discordant with your personality as I knew it that I never realized or conceived that your frustration could be tied to something larger."

Jamie / Friend / Austin

CHAPTER 5

The Juice

Obtaining hormones essentially became a quest to find a decent doctor without having to do a ton of therapy. As was the case with top surgery, the benefits felt naively negligible to me. Therapy was both expensive and time consuming, and I didn't need a stranger to sign off that I was actually transgender. I understood what I was doing to my body, and after my recent surgery, I was even more desperate to align the rest of my body with my mind. Without breasts, I was more often addressed as "sir" by strangers and then forced to deal with their spiraling, frantic apologies when they realized their "mistake." Hormones had to happen, pronto. I would deal with the emotional upheaval later.

After many phone calls, I found a doctor who required no therapy letter. It became clear why almost immediately after entering her office; the care was certainly not up to par. In response to my explanation of the existing phallic medical device options for men, she responded, "They can do that nowadays?!" clearly flabbergasted. *Not a good sign.* I was stepping into the beginning of the rest of my life and this "professional" had no actual knowledge of a significant potential part of the transgender experience. Her ignorance was mortifying, her overall demeanor seemingly rushed and slightly irritated. Each question I had was met with an impersonal pamphlet or the generic response, "Everyone is different." She had minimal understanding of acceptable hormone levels, timelines for expected changes, and ignorantly asked me if my nipples had been tattooed on. I figured someone in her line of care would be congratulatory and supportive of my recent top surgery results. *Apparently not.* She handed me one last pamphlet on "Egg Freezing Options," and I was done. My ability to have biological children would essentially go out the window the moment I started hormones, and the doctor showed no ability to appreciate the significance of that life-altering reality. I burst into tears the moment the clinic doors shut behind me. I couldn't bring myself to take the prescription to the pharmacy no matter how badly I wanted to start testosterone. I never wanted to see that horrendous woman ever again.

Following that letdown of an appointment, I found a new borderline satisfactory doctor who required only one therapy letter. After the last experience, I figured that requiring a letter was a sign that they were at least concerned about the patients' well-being. The new doctor's website boasted a holistic approach, and the waiting room was a welcoming mix of pet birds and his quirky wife. I was on edge and the environment made me feel at ease. I adore birds and the friendly wife was more than happy to chat about it. My meeting with the doctor carried the same casual ambiance. He confidently answered all of my questions, and even went as far as to claim, "You are not sick, we are just fixing something that went wrong." I appreciated his efforts to validate my decision to start hormones, although it did feel a tad forced. I couldn't tell you what he actually thought.

The doctor went on to further explain the effects of testosterone that were irreversible. "Once you start, your voice will drop and hair will grow in places it hasn't before. Your hairline can recede due to the triggering of male pattern baldness. Do the men on your mom's side have hair loss?" he asked.

"I'm not sure," I said shakily. "I'll have to check with her."

He continued, "Just something to be aware of. All of these things are permanent."

I nodded in understanding. I was terrified, but this was the only path forward. I would take the bad with the good, regardless of how that looked. The doctor touched on some of the non-permanent changes, including body fat redistribution and a potential increase in red blood cell count, and I was on my way, prescription in hand. "Some of these things all depend on the person," he said as I exited the office. "The changes should be done in two to three years tops."

A few days later, I scheduled my first set of labs. The doctor had to know where my baseline testosterone levels were at so we could ensure my health stayed on track. I was terrified. Rachel and I used to donate blood in high school to get out of class, but after one traumatic visit during my senior year, I had been unable to return. "You have really rubbery veins," the nurse had told me as she dug around my arm for an eternity trying to find an entry point. My arm was bruised for weeks, and I had desperately avoided blood draws ever since. I was sweating as I entered the clinic in Austin, knowing there was no other choice if I wanted my hormones.

Thankfully, the nurse did a better job than the one from years prior. She made no observation regarding my "rubbery veins" and performed the blood draw with ease. The doctor emailed me a few days later to let me know I was good to go. Interestingly, my baseline levels were far below average for a woman. "A third of the typical levels," the doctor suggested. I had a lot of catching up to do, and it was time to get started.

Matt and Constance sat with me in the living room while I stared at the needle and vial. It was June 17, 2015, and it was now or never. I was about to take the biggest step of my life, and my mind was suffocated with fear of the unknown. The goal was to "pass," or in other words be perceived as the gender I wished to present as, and I was desperately unsure if that was going to be feasible for me. I worried that my face was too feminine and wouldn't masculinize enough to be convincingly male. I was convinced that the curves of my hips and thighs were too prominent, and my meager height of 5'5" would ultimately give me away. My goal was to not stand out anymore, and I couldn't stand the thought of exacerbating the straight world's confusion over my gender identity.

Matt suddenly interjected and asked what I was waiting for.

I was thankful for his help in stopping the "what if" web from spinning any further in my mind. "The injection will feel the same whether you do it now or wait another twenty minutes," he said as his kind eyes smiled at me. He didn't know, of course, that the shot itself wasn't the scary part. I was scared of blood draws, not needles. I prepped the syringe and pushed the needle into my thigh as hard as I could. We all laughed together as I winced in pain. "I probably shouldn't have injected myself like this is a lifesaving EpiPen shot," I said to them both. *Albeit, most likely still lifesaving.* My thigh was bruised and sore for the next week while I anxiously waited to "feel" the hormones.

The first of many

A week later, I called my parents before heading into the theater to see *Jurassic World* with Constance. I had waited on account of the guilt. My mom was more on board, or better prepared, than my dad, but neither of them deserved this. They had showered me in unconditional love since the day I was born, and now I was taking away their only daughter. It was all so helpless. I had done everything to avoid taking Lauren away from them, and this decision set in stone that their daughter would be gone forever. We had discussed it in the car on the way back from Plano, but now it was real. *Surely, having a transgender son would be more complicated than having a lesbian daughter.* There was no other way. Inevitably, the introduction of James would accompany the loss of Lauren and any of the remaining "normalcy" that was associated with her.

"I just wanted to let you know that I started hormones last week," I said hesitantly, rubbing the bruise on my thigh. I knew my parents wouldn't be angry, but I still wasn't sure how they would respond. They did what any parents should do and asked me how I was feeling. Nothing felt all that different yet, so there wasn't much to relay. We exchanged "I love yous" and hung up. As the call clicked off, the loneliness rolled in like a tidal wave. *How many other kids have to tell their parents that they just started hormones?* Thankfully, the dinosaurs served as a sufficient distraction for the rest of the evening. I would deal with the isolation later.

Over the next month, I anxiously tracked every feeling in my body. I could sense the trembles of a figurative tidal wave building deep within. Something big was coming. *An impending doom.* I was destroying a perfectly healthy body, and I would surely pay for that somehow. The guilt ran hot through me, my body finally taking a stand about a week before the one-month mark. My system wasted no time in violently letting me know that it didn't like what was happening. Menstruation had always been horrendous, but nothing compared to this final hurrah. Estrogen and testosterone were waging war inside of me, and I was a useless bystander. Shivers ran up and down my body, occasionally accompanied by an unbearable heat, while my lower stomach cramped with more intensity than it ever had before. I left work crying, in immense pain, both emotional and physical. I called my dad for a reprieve. "I think I've made a mistake," I said, sobbing in my car. "Maybe I'm not transgender after all," I had concluded. Something was obviously wrong. I could hear my dad's palpable surprise at the end of the line. This was his moment to get his daughter back. "Give yourself time. There's a lot going on right now," he said supportively. "Don't make any rash decisions." (*Thank you, Dad*).

A week after the period from hell abated, I was still James. At that point, I made the decision to finally tell the staff at work. My identity was clearly not relevant to my career, but it would be far too disruptive to say nothing. My fears that I wouldn't "pass" had already started to dissipate. The changes were happening almost too quickly for me to keep up with, and there wasn't much time left before things would definitely start to get awkward. I reached out to our Human Resource site representative, Shirley, to set up a meeting.

Shirley was a kind, gentle, middle-aged woman who had already proven herself to be wonderfully supportive. She was poorly equipped to answer most work-related questions, but somehow had the ally vibes down pat. She had even been supportive in response to my recent request for the installation of a gender-neutral bathroom on site. "This is becoming the norm across workplaces, restaurants, and stores," I had explained to her with conviction one afternoon. "You're right, Lauren. I'll speak to the site supervisor right away." Sure enough, a few weeks later, a construction crew was knocking down a wall to make way for the new space. I couldn't believe how easy it had been. Some of my transgender friends had experienced vastly different treatment in their workplaces.

The day of my meeting with Shirley, I started by acknowledging the installation of the bathroom. "Thank you so much for making this happen. I'm sure this will help many people, myself included, feel more comfortable here at work." She smiled in return. "Of course, Lauren. Thank you for your patience while they got it set up." I smiled back, my heart suddenly tightening as I braced for our next topic. "Speaking of being more comfortable at work," I paused, "there is something else I need to talk to you about." She nodded to encourage my continued ownership of the conversation. "I started hormones about a month ago, and I think it's time I tell the staff." Her facial expression remained the same, warm and welcoming, and not at all surprised. We had discussed possible FMLA for my recent surgery, and the bathroom dealio, and I was growing more masculine by the day. I often wondered if my coworkers noticed how much I was in her office, my little feet dangling as I sat in one of Shirley's tall chairs.

"First of all, congratulations," she responded encouragingly when I stopped speaking. I was thankful Shirley's allyship had remained intact. "You must feel so happy," she said, beaming back at me. I assured her that I did, although the feelings were a lot to manage. "I couldn't possibly understand, but I'm here if you ever want to chat," she assured me. I thanked her and we moved on to discussing how on earth we would tell the staff. "My only concern is making them feel like we are strong-arming them into accepting this," Shirley said. "It may be better if a Human Resource or upper management presence is absent from the room during the announcement." I looked at her, concerned. "Would you be comfortable with that?" she inquired.

I sat silent for a moment, considering the suggestion as I fixated on the tree outside her window. I envied how free its leaves looked, rustling in the wind. A sheer contrast to my current reality. "It's overwhelming to imagine telling all of those people by myself, but I totally understand what you're saying." Considering the gracious, albeit necessary, recent bathroom upgrade, I agreed to the request. Shirley was doing all she could to support me, and I appreciated her sincere efforts. I was the first employee to transition at the company, and this was new to everyone. I would be slow to judge how she or the rest of management responded to such unknowns.

The following week, I sat at the front of the conference room while thirty pairs of eyes stared back at me, anxious to hear my announcement. This was the first meeting of three scheduled for that day. A few of my close friends at work already knew, so I steadily held eye contact with them as I shared the news with everyone else. My voice shook as I said the words I had thought about for years. I focused my approach around giving and asking for respect. I wasn't going to stand for discrimination, but I also had to accept that some folks were inevitably going to struggle with this. I delicately stated that I respected the fact that this was everyone else's workplace too. I had no intent of forcing them to honor my request if they did not feel comfortable. These people didn't have the option to steer clear of me if they truly thought I was the devil reincarnated.

"Hey, you stole my name!" exclaimed one of my male coworkers from the back of the room during the first meeting. He was a James Bradley too. Everyone erupted in laughter, and I wanted to jump up and hug him for breaking the ice so effectively. A select few of the staff sat silently staring off into the distance, but that was fine by me. I assumed they felt overwhelmed after meeting a transgender person for the first time. I ignored my persistent discomfort and concluded each meeting with one specific request: "Please do not ask me any questions that you would not want to be asked yourself." *In other words, please do not ask me about my genitals.* I knew it was a possibility if I didn't at least indirectly address it. I explained that I was happy to answer questions and help educate folks whenever appropriate, but the line would be drawn there. Everyone nodded as a sign of their understanding. A wave of relief washed over me when the third meeting ended.

In unison, Constance told the kids at her school. She was a teacher at a school nearby, and I visited often. The students knew me as Lauren, Constance's girlfriend, and we had to prepare them for the upcoming changes. Constance gathered them outside, letting them know that she had something to tell them. An exciting announcement for the kiddos. *Are we getting candy?* "You know my girlfriend, Lauren?" she asked the group. "Yes," they all responded in unison. "Well, Lauren is now a boy and his name is James," she continued on, bluntly. "Okay!" they exclaimed, and ran off back to the playground. They literally didn't miss a beat. It's incredible, and horribly sad, how learned hate changes some adults.

That night, Constance and I met up with my friend group at our local bar, Cheer Up Charlies. The space was an indoor/outdoor mostly queer bar, with a handful of easygoing straight people and themed music nights that absolutely slayed. Rihanna versus Beyonce was my favorite. You could fill buckets with the sweat pouring off that dance floor. Considering we were celebrating on a school night, the music was kept to a minimum. We all piled into a long wooden picnic table, bantering back and forth over cold beer and delicious food from the nearby food trucks. There were about ten of us, although the entire group was much larger. I had separated from my initial friend group years prior following the problematic decisions made in my romantic life. The new crew, otherwise known as the Gaggle, had been formed on the basis of queers who loved brunch.

As I shared the day's successes, the entire table responded with glee and congratulatory adoration. My journey leading up to this day, tequila shot in hand, had been a difficult one.

My friends had seen me struggle at first with the decision of top surgery and ultimately, to pursue hormones. We hugged and danced and hugged some more. The celebrations went late into the night, and I will never forget the way in which they embraced James. It was as if they had been waiting to meet him too.

CHAPTER 6

Coming Out, Again

Over the following month or so, amid many more Cheer Ups hangouts, I delicately figured out how to come out to everyone else in my life. My extended relatives and family friends were not yet aware, and my mom was eager to help me figure out how to tell them. We hoped it wouldn't come as a surprise, although it was still nerve-racking not knowing how people might react. A majority of these people were straight and cisgender, and coming out this time was going to be slightly more complicated than just showing up at Thanksgiving with a new girlfriend. Mom and I felt a letter would be best. In retrospect, I'm not sure why we kept up with using "she" and "Lauren" throughout it.

Dear Family & Friends

Please see the letter from Lauren below.

However difficult this is for us to get our minds around—we have to try and understand the emotional and physical turmoil that Lauren has been dealing with for many years, and put that ahead of how we feel about the reality of losing a lovely daughter and a sister—at least as we knew her outwardly. Inside, the same lovely person still exists, whom we will always love and admire more than words can say.

We have to think that this may not come as a surprise to many of you, even though you may have not seen Lauren in quite a while. Her transformation thus far has become more and more noticeable over the last couple of years, even without the recent changes.

We are dealing with this the best we can and giving her all the love and support she needs.

Please feel free to email Lauren.
Carol, Stephen & Jon xxx

Hello beloved friends and family,

I feel it is time to come out for the second time in my life, this time to the truest version of myself. This has been an extremely difficult road at times, but I have never felt happiness like this in my life now that this journey has officially started. Over the past few months, I have begun my transition from female to male. I'm not sure if this will come as a surprise to any of you, but it is something that has been eating away at me for years. My most recent memories of feeling this way stem back to childhood, but as an adult, I have been struggling to make this decision for the past five years. I know that there are many fears associated with what the outcome of this may be or the difficult path I am now embarking on, but I can sincerely tell you, nothing can be worse than the conflict that I have felt inside. I have reached a point in my adult life where I am ready to take this challenge on if it means I can spend the rest of my life feeling like the real me. This is the happiness I am talking about. I can have all the things in the world, but without inner happiness, it all feels quite meaningless at times.

I had my breast removal surgery in April and my recovery has been fantastic. This was ultimately the deciding factor. I knew that I would know then if I was going to carry on to the next step of hormones or be happy as I was following that physical alteration. Unfortunately, it was more securing than ever in my decision to continue my transition. I was hoping it would be an easy fix, but this is the hand I've been dealt, and I've come to realize that there is no easy fix. This is most definitely not a choice; it is a necessity. I have been on hormones for about five weeks now, and I feel fantastic. There have been a few ups and downs, but each day I get closer to being the person I've always seen in my head. Thankfully, work has been extremely understanding and all of my coworkers are now aware of my transition. They even put in a gender-neutral bathroom for me! There is always the fear that this will affect future job opportunities and relationships, but if one is not happy with themselves, there really is no point seeking happiness elsewhere. This may be the most important lesson I've learned in my adult life so far.

I have chosen the name James Bradley as James has always been close to my heart and Bradley is one of my favorite boys' names. It most certainly is weird having to choose a new name for yourself! I have come out to my close friends and thankfully, my partner is overwhelmingly supportive. I believe the process should take about two years before I can exist comfortably as a "passing" male, but these small changes in my appearance are already starting to make a difference in my day-to-day comfort. I love you all and would appreciate your support through this challenging journey. I will still be the same person that Lauren was, only hopefully a little more handsome ;) I can't wait to feel the happiness that is to come and to share that person with all of you.

Love always,
James

The support and love that came pouring in from most of the recipients was incredible. A few family friends never responded or acknowledged the change, but I was mostly upset with their lack of interest for my parents' sake. It's not every day that a parent has to grieve the loss of a daughter that is being replaced with a son, and they deserved better from some of their so-called friends. I couldn't understand the lack of support, regardless of their potential negative opinions on transgender people. Even my ninety-year-old grandparents were on board. They emailed back immediately, with both of my parents copied in. "We hope that things end up the way you feel happiest and you will continue to enjoy both your job and your social life with all your friends. Life is for living; we are only here once and we must make the most of it." Their only request was that they could call me Jamesie instead of James. "It's just a little softer," they elaborated. I gladly obliged, thankful that this was the only thing they were worried about. *TAKE NOTES, FAMILY MEMBERS AND FRIENDS OF TRANSGENDER PEOPLE. If my ninety-year-old grandparents can accept a transgender person, so can you.*

The best of the best

As we embraced the responses from our family and friends, I enthusiastically drafted my long-awaited Facebook announcement to inform everyone else in my life. There were many more friends and acquaintances I'd collected over the years, and I couldn't wait to share my update with them. Once perfected, I hit POST and anxiously waited for my notifications to start pinging. *Who would be the first to like it? Would there be any less-than-congratulatory comments?* The response was overwhelming, to say the least. I had never felt so loved in my life.

James Bennett
July 28, 2015 · Austin, TX ·

I've always thought about this moment and felt concerned about how hard it would be to come out to other people as transgender. However, now that this journey has begun, I have realized that the hardest part was coming out to myself. I have finally embarked on my journey of transition from female to male. I have known that I should have been born male for the majority of my life and have spent years trying to accept the fact that I would have to spend my life as a woman. In my 25th year of life, I have realized that this is no longer feasible for me. I have let go of my fears of the unknown and allowed myself to begin this journey with everything I have. It really came down to the fact that I didn't want to spend my life surrounded by happiness that I couldn't fully enjoy because I wasn't truly happy with myself. I am so excited to feel comfortable in my own skin and share this new found love for myself with all of those around me. I am so fortunate for the love and support that I have received thus far from my family and close friends, and I hope that I continue to feel this acceptance. I know that this will be a tough journey, as it already has been, but I know that being happy with myself will lead to the happiest life possible. I would like to be addressed with he/him pronouns from this point forward and by my chosen name of James.

Thank you to all of the people who have supported me and allowed me to get to this place today. I am forever grateful.

- James Bradley Bennett

Facebook post

The only outstanding obstacle to "completing" my second coming out process was my younger brother, Jon. He and I had oscillated between getting along or not for most of our adult lives, and my identity issues only served to exacerbate the tension. I was jealous of him for being male, and he was jealous of me for reasons I've never truly understood. Unfortunately, the closer I got to being James, the less he was able to compassionately respond. It was a confusing, hurtful 180 from his treatment of me as a lesbian sister. He had always supported me, often getting angry with his jock friends if they said anything offensive about gay people. Me becoming his brother somehow shifted the paradigm completely. It hadn't gone well since the first mention of the possibility.

In December of the prior year, I was home for a visit and asked Jon if he wanted to drive me to the gas station to buy cigarettes. He and I both smoked for far too many years into our twenties. "Sure!" he exclaimed, excited to take me out in his new BMW. We both shared a love for fancy cars that were definitely too fast for either of us to drive responsibly. As we drove, listening to our favorite song, "Poppin' Them Thangs" by G-Unit, I nervously brought up the real reason for our errand.

"I've been wanting to talk to you about something," I started out cautiously. "You know how I have surgery in April of next year?"

He responded kindly, "Yes, of course. How could I forget?"

I held my breath, much more nervous to continue with the next line. "Well, it's possible I may decide to start hormones one day. I'm not sure yet. I still need to see how I feel after surgery," I continued on.

"Okay. That makes sense," he said matter-of-factly.

We promptly arrived at the gas station, awkwardly pausing our conversation. He ran inside to grab our favorites with cash provided by me. I sat nervously in the car, anticipating his return. I had no idea how he would react to the rest of the conversation. He had gotten angry at me in the past for changing my name to Lauren James on Facebook and we'd never resolved it. James was his middle name, after all. His friends had apparently brought it up, blindsiding him and subsequently leading to a typical volatile blow up between us. *Sorry?*

Jon quickly returned, smiling as he tore the plastic off the cigarette packages. He jumped in the car, causing it to sink slightly as he got situated. He was a big guy, 6'4" with legs and arms that reminded me of a praying mantis. He never liked when I called him that as a joke though. I looked back over at him, scanning his tall, strong frame with jealousy. He could barely fit in the seat, and I had enough room for an oversized toddler to sit next to me.

I pushed back into the conversation to break my damaging train of thought. "Mom told me a story a few years ago about what happened when she was pregnant with me. She thought she was having a boy and they had the name James picked out for me." My heart froze as I looked over at him. Jon was smart enough to know what was coming next.

"Okay . . ." he responded, causing me to feel slightly irritated by his inability to understand the significance of the information I had just divulged.

"If I do start hormones, I would like to change my name to James. It is the only name that feels right to me. I considered Bradley, but I really don't want people to call me Brad. It's too bro-y and it doesn't fit." He stared off, not really saying much.

I kept talking. I had to get it all out. "Is it okay with you if I do choose James? You don't have to decide today, we have time." I looked back over at him, desperate for a read. His face never gave much away.

"I'll think about it," he responded somewhat dismissively.

I thanked him anyway. We turned the music back up and resumed filling our lungs with smoke. It was clear I wasn't going to get my answer that day.

After surgery and the realization that I was in fact transgender, I was still without an answer from my brother. I had already started hormones, and I didn't know what to do. I couldn't spend my life with a name I didn't love. This was my chance to start over. On a walk with my parents one afternoon, I explained my dilemma. My mom was angered by the disclosure, my dad mostly silent. "He can be so selfish," she said, fuming. "I know, but I don't want to hurt him," I responded, kicking rocks along the dirt path. We walked silently for a few more paces until my mom offered her final opinion. "You know what, it's your life. You should just do what feels right." I nodded in agreement. Her only request was that I tell Jon I had chosen James before he found out elsewhere. "Good call," I said in agreement.

I called Jon the next week on my way home from work. The phone call started off reasonably well. We caught up on each other's lives, work, and relationships, but once we shifted onto the topic of my transition, it all fell apart. Jon was furious with me for "taking" the name James, regardless of the fact that I had asked him before finalizing the decision. He had left me without an answer, so I moved forward with my life accordingly.

"I asked you six months ago!" I screamed back at him, seething with his inability to think outside of himself. "I told you all about Mom's pregnancy and her selection of the name James for me before I was born. I don't understand how you can't appreciate the significance of that. You don't even go by James," I said, my voice growing more forceful with each sentence.

"What am I supposed to do, tell my friends that I have a brother instead of a sister now?!" he exclaimed with exasperation. He had been so supportive and protective over me as his gay sister, yet somehow, me transitioning was drastically different. I struggled to understand.

"Yes, exactly," I responded with as much conviction as I could muster.

He clearly didn't appreciate my tone, and the call escalated quickly after that until it ended with one of us abruptly hanging up.

I walked into my house from my car and proceeded to kick my dresser so hard it shattered.

"Are you okay?!" Matt called to me from the kitchen.

"No," I responded, filled with frustration. There was nothing I could do. Jon and I didn't speak for months after, and I worried that our relationship was as irreparable as my dresser.

CHAPTER 7

The Australia Tattoo

The task of coming out eventually abated, and I was left to manage the intense effects of puberty round two. For the first year or so, *I thought this would make things easier* ran laps around my brain starting almost as soon as I awoke. I had a brief few seconds of peace before I remembered that I was transitioning. After that, there was seemingly no option to hit the pause button; the discomfort just kept on coming. As I went about my morning routine, a wave of dread would roll over me, and things would progressively get worse from there. My new baseline brought me closer to what I would expect it feels like to be a teenage boy: awkward, frantic, and out of place.

"James, you have chest hair now!" or "You've really bulked up" became commonplace comments day to day, even at work. People suddenly felt it acceptable to comment on every aspect of my physical appearance. *How else could they possibly acknowledge I was transitioning?* I tried to remain grateful that they were at least supportive and validating of my progress, but my discomfort ran rampant. I thanked them regardless. These people had no idea how I was actually feeling, but a lack of support would have been much worse. Behind the "amazing" physical changes was a mind barely able to keep up. Everything I had grown accustomed to for twenty-five years had slowly begun to slip away.

Hair grew almost everywhere on my body, except where it began to recede on my head. A plague of cystic acne ran rampant across both my face and my back, and my voice deepened in a way that made passing a reality for the first time. My hunger spiked so significantly that the need to satisfy my appetite became surprisingly disruptive. I gained 15 pounds in a matter of months and grew physically stronger than I had ever been seemingly overnight. I was suddenly unable to button most of my shirts and my pants pulled tighter in different areas from what I was used to. I struggled constantly to embrace my larger body mass even though I had waited anxiously for years to look more masculine. As a woman, I had been taught that any increase in mass was a bad thing. I had learned to associate "bigger" with "fatter." As a male, society expected me to be bigger than I was as a female, and I was forced to completely rewire my brain as a result. *This is a good thing,* I would tell myself when I felt self-conscious. *It is "acceptable" for you to have broader shoulders and a thicker torso. You are replacing your pants due to an increase in thigh muscle, not an increase in fat.* I struggled incessantly to process all the changes while simply trying to live my life in the background. There were layers upon layers of foreign anxieties sprouting up all over my new body.

To make matters worse, everything felt *so fucking intense*. I was eternally frustrated with the discomfort, and testosterone had quickly escalated my temper to an unprecedented level. I had previously had a bad temper, but this was unmatched. The figurative damper that kept my "temper flame" in check during my female years was gone in an instant. The flame ran rampant, and I suddenly felt completely out of control. All my years of effort to control that flame were foiled in a matter of months. I struggled to keep myself together at work when people were frustrating, and minor inconveniences like traffic became a source of completely ridiculous meltdowns. The feeling was unbearable. I was no longer the calm, collected adult I strived to be, and I barely recognized myself. One afternoon at work, one of my staff asked for her desk to be moved as her cube neighbor "chewed too loudly," and I could hardly hold myself together on account of my anger. I would have done anything in the moment for that insignificant annoyance to be the greatest concern in my life. I began to resent everyone and everything.

In parallel, my relationship with Constance began to slowly crumble. She and I had weathered a few fights prior, but after I started hormones, every disagreement we faced was exacerbated by the emotional rollercoaster I had recently boarded. It was a recipe for disaster, and I was unable to discern between where my inner turmoil ended and our standard relationship troubles began. We broke up and got back together constantly, my anger spiking dangerously each time we argued. My poor dad transformed into my therapist, constantly encouraging me to do what was best for me. His advice never changed after the first split. Constance and I were not meant for each other and it was obvious. Regardless, he would inevitably receive another phone call announcing our recent resolve. "This time will be different," I would naively assure him. It would take years before I finally stopped falling back into her arms.

In addition to my turbulent emotional state and relationship troubles, the added stressors of finding the right hormone level and maintaining adequate care only served to exacerbate my anger. The second doctor, the one with birds in his waiting room, never quite came through after the first appointment. He spoke in a strangely transphobic manner about his own child's identity during our second appointment, and it took us many isolating months to figure out the right amount of testosterone for me to inject. Although I understood the necessity of trial and error, the doctor showed no compassion regarding the costs or emotional ramifications of this experiment. My free time was spent partaking in labs and appointments, costing hundreds of dollars each month. I felt like some kind of lab rat in an overtly expensive clinical trial, and I was desperate for the doctor to care more than he did.

About six weeks after starting T, I emailed him, feeling concerned with the level of anxiety I was experiencing. The doctor responded that I was due for my two months labs, coupled with the blanket statement, "Looks like we have something to talk about, eh?" A week or so later, after facing my fears of blood draws for the second time, the doctor emailed me again. "Hey Lauren, so your testo is 1024. You can either inject the same amount every 8 days or cut your dose to 0.4ml and continue to do it every 6 days. This should get you back to around 800." I could not for the life of me understand why he was still calling me Lauren, and I was immediately bothered by his lack of concern regarding my T level. I was 85.3x where I had started. *No wonder I was feeling so fucking crazy.* I immediately lowered my dose, only to find that my mood was significantly declining days before I would be due for my next shot. I messaged him again, pouring my heart out. "So, inject the 0.5ml every 6 days instead of every week. That ought to fix things," was all I got in response. *Fix things? What does that even mean?* I was angry and eager for something better.

After one more colossal show of his apathy, I knew it was time to move on. I had asked the doctor to write a letter explaining my mismatching documentation for an upcoming international work trip to England at the end of 2015. I was extremely nervous to face customs and hoped that an explanation from my healthcare professional would work in my favor. The doctor seemed on board with the simple task, only to confuse which way I was transitioning in *two* separate instances. "To whom it may concern, James Bennett, aka Lauren Bennett, is a patient of mine who will be traveling internationally, leaving on July the second of this year. He is currently in transition from the male to female sex so there will be a discrepancy between his photos on his passport and other IDs, and his current appearance." I informed the doctor of his error, he "corrected" it, and proceeded to leave the same letter under his mat for me to pick up the next day. I was furious when I realized, barely able to stay under the speed limit on my way home. After blaming the second error on his wife, I was done. I went to the airport with no letter and vowed to find a new doctor the moment I got home. I couldn't stand the thought of giving that man another penny.

I sifted through shitty doctors for months before I found one that I liked. (*Kind Clinic, you are amazing.*) As was the case with the first doc, the level of care from a majority of the so-called hormone replacement therapy experts I met with before I found the clinic was terribly inadequate. I started to feel like a cash cow, clearly being taken advantage of. The doctors never seemed able to comprehend how significant hormones were, and they unreasonably made me start my labs over each time. I was furious and unable to keep up with the financial drain. *In what world can doctors not use prior medical records or recent lab work?* I seemingly could never get a straight answer to my questions, and each doctor had drastically different opinions on acceptable hormone levels and expected effects of testosterone. I was constantly upset and exhausted, desperate to find something that felt stable and secure. To make matters worse, if I ever saw a doctor for a reason unrelated to my transition, they were typically unable to speak to how testosterone would affect any other aspect of my health. "You just never know with hormones," they would say. *No one else has to do this*, played over and over in my head. I had never felt more alone.

As I battled through the dire isolation, the onslaught of unexpected changes never stopped. They just kept on coming, never letting me up for air. I used to cry when I felt frustrated or angry, and suddenly, I felt frustrated and angry most of the time, but with no tears to help release the emotion. I was exasperated with the loss of that therapeutic relief. I needed it now more than ever, and I could no longer access it even when I wanted to. Emotional situations, excluding explosive break-ups with Constance, left me without feeling, and I couldn't make sense of how my mind was acting. I would sit there, almost emotionless, unable to process my feelings. My mind would often drift off and daydream about what I would do after the situation subsided. *As soon as this is over, you can go biking*, my mind would tell me. I was disappointed with myself for being so avoidant. It all felt so painfully foreign to me.

If I ever did cry, it was typically unexpected and in the reverse order of what I was used to. Prior to transition, when I saw something awful like that Sarah McLachlan ASPCA commercial, I would feel sad and then I would start crying. After the introduction of testosterone, the same commercial would come on, my eyes would well with tears, and then I would register that I felt sad. It was as if my physical response was accessing a part of my emotion that I was subconsciously pushing away. The emotional response had momentarily been stored somewhere else that I was unaware of. "Maybe it's some type of Pavlovian response," my friend suggested one day when I opened up about it. I was comforted by the thought initially, but even that was ripped away when I had the same reaction a few days later watching a movie I had never seen before. *Nothing made sense.*

I was suddenly a blunted, greyer version of my former self. A colorless terrain where a complex landscape of beautiful colors once existed. I once succeeded in environments that required my attention to be split in multiple different directions, and suddenly, I preferred to work on singular tasks. There was no more intricate web of thoughts, just a single track of nothingness. I frequently had to say out loud, "Hold on, I can't do two things at once," when I was engaging with another person and my attention was compromised. The drastic changes made me question if I really knew who I was in the first place. I considered that the changes might be due to my increasing age, but ultimately had to accept that I would never be able to discern the difference. *Is this just what becoming an adult is?* The rug had been pulled out from under me, and I was endlessly exhausted. I was nothing more than a big ball of goo, completely susceptible to changing every aspect of who I was, both physically and emotionally, with each injection of testosterone. *Maybe there was no "self" after all. Maybe we are all just a series of chemical reactions caused by whatever hormone balance we contain.*

With the loss of footing, I couldn't stop questioning integral parts of my understanding of the world. I had always believed that men barely expressed emotion and cried less than women because society considered emotion a sign of weakness. Suddenly, I wasn't so sure. *What if, like me, they can't cry?* I wasn't trying to feel less emotion, I just did. *Was this all just caused by testosterone?* It was impossible to know. From there, I found myself at the center of jokes about men not being able to multitask. I was on track to be the person whose wife couldn't get his attention during a football game. *Ew.* I didn't know where and when it was going to stop. I worried that my understanding of the world would continue to deteriorate as my transition progressed. Puberty 2.0 was effectively recording over my existing mind. I may not have liked how my body changed after the first bout, but at least I didn't have twenty-five years of beliefs and self-perspective to contend with that time around.

When I traveled back home for reprieve, I often left feeling worse than when I arrived. I enjoyed the excitement of seeing old friends from high school and college, but interactions with family friends followed a vastly different trajectory. During Thanksgiving and Christmas gatherings, our family friends would stare at me, their eyes filled with curiosity. The physical changes were immense, and my new body wasn't something easily ignored. "James looks so different," our friends would tell my parents after I left. I never understood what they expected in response. *Obviously?*

I hated the thought of my parents feeling ashamed, although they never once voiced the sentiment. I longed for someone to ask how they were feeling or provide them with some inkling of support that I couldn't. No one could possibly understand the effects a transition has on family dynamics. To my parents and my direct family as a whole, my transition meant a daughter, granddaughter, and sister was being replaced with a son, grandson, and brother. Much more jarring than a family friend morphing from female to male.

I did all I could to manage through the discomfort and guilt, but would often return to Austin feeling more isolated than ever. I was so painfully struggling, and my parents could only do so much to counter it. The never-ending barrage of self-doubt and confusion continued to consume aspects of my day-to-day life, constant and relentless. I was in my late twenties with a career to build, relationships to maintain, and a social life I so desperately wanted to enjoy. I continuously tried and failed to push away the unsteadiness, but was only able to obtain intermittent success.

When I was around unfamiliar people, I worried constantly that they would know I was transgender even though I had been passing for months. I only got called "ma'am" occasionally on the phone, but after I learned to project my words from my chest to make my voice sound deeper, even that stopped happening. I did everything I could to feel more at ease, but to no avail. I tried to dress differently, but I hated loose clothing. I worked on holding my body in a less effeminate way, but it felt awkward and ultimately made me more unsure of myself. I continued to seek out haircuts that masculinized my face, but the moment my hair grew back out, I worried I looked too feminine again. I couldn't escape my daily reality, and I feared that my life would never feel comfortable.

As a testament to my discomfort and fear that people in the straight world would "know" I was transgender, I eventually chose to have my bigender tattoo covered up. I had been so proud of it years earlier, but with the recent physical changes, all it did was cause me anguish. If people noticed it, they would have more of a reason to stare at me, and I couldn't have that. When I was cycling, I would obsess over whether people in their cars were looking at me after being drawn in by my unusual tattoo. I didn't want to give them any more reason to inspect my body in my already revealing spandex. *Surely, they will notice my lack of a bulge.* I would watch the light impatiently until it turned green and I could peddle away from their potential stares once again.

I settled on Australia after brainstorming all the large black blobs I could cover the symbol with. The country outline was the perfect size, and there was no way I was ever going to want to hide that part of myself. (Spoiler: I had it removed eight years later.) I felt such shame as the tattoo artist streaked black lines over the symbol I had once been so adamant about feeling absolutely right. It ended up looking like shit and my mind cruelly convinced me that this was my punishment. *Mom was right. You should have been more sure before you permanently marked yourself, idiot.*

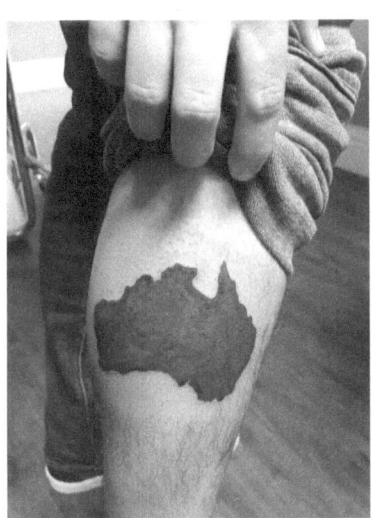

Not my best decision

CHAPTER 8

Jasmine's Lyft

As I battled through the seemingly never ending physical and emotional discomfort, my place in society was also shifting in a drastic way. With the sudden change in my appearance, I simultaneously lost queer visibility and gained male privilege all at the same time. Prior to transition, my feminine curves, short haircut, and masculine clothing made me recognizable to any queer person I met. If I saw a stranger like me in public, we would smile and exchange head nods. *I see you*, we would signal. The interaction needn't go beyond that. The approving gesture acknowledged our sameness without words; an effortless recognition of community.

With each shot of testosterone, the once frequent, beautiful points of effortless connection slowly started to fade. The changes were subtle at first, but the more masculine my body became, the quicker my feeling of belonging diminished. The smiles and head nods stopped, and I was suddenly a stranger in a place that used to feel like home. Even with my shirt off at the pool or beach, other queer people would often not even realize that I was transgender. The shift was devastating. When my friend group introduced new people, I felt an overt internal pressure to justify my presence. I looked like a white, cisgender man now, and I desperately wanted them to know that I wasn't. I couldn't possibly be the "other" after all this time. I had depth of experience and was just as queer as them. My soul was screaming to be recognized. *I'm one of you! Why don't you see me anymore?*

Simultaneously, any and all sexual harassment from straight, cisgender men completely stopped. Now that they perceived me as "one of them," I was suddenly respected in a way that felt powerful beyond measure. Men no longer objectified my body or flirted with me in unwanted ways. I could suddenly choose to walk home alone at 2am without having to weigh out the risks of doing so. I no longer had to worry about having cell service when I went hiking, and I never had to have an exit strategy planned. My body became an asset rather than a conduit for potential harassment or violence, and I felt more valuable than I ever had. A stark contrast to my restaurant days in my early twenties.

I will never forget the first time I experienced this overt undeserved privilege firsthand. I was about six months into my transition, and my boss had asked me to attend a meeting in her place last minute. She was unable to make it and knew I was knowledgeable enough to speak on the subject. I was nervous and unsure of myself, but excited nonetheless. I craved any opportunity to put myself out there professionally. I grabbed my suit jacket and set off to find the conference room. Upon entering, I was met with at least fifteen pairs of eyes staring back at me. Eighty percent of the room was male, and I was terrified. The tables were arranged in a U shape and there was one seat left, right at the bottom center of the U. Great. As I sat down, I noticed that the eyes hadn't left me. I worried that they knew I was transgender, but quickly reassured myself how unlikely that was.

The individual speaking quickly stopped and asked me to introduce myself. I was taken aback by how soon after I had entered the room I was introduced. The timing was unusual and made me feel important. I introduced myself, the room acknowledged me, and the speaker resumed speaking. After some discussion, my contribution to the subject was next. I was reintroduced and asked to explain how my team was involved in the process they were discussing. As I spoke, all eyes remained on me. No one looked away or appeared disinterested. They asked me questions and nodded with satisfaction when I answered. The men spoke over the women and they engaged with me in a way I had never experienced. It was the first time in my entire life I can ever remember feeling respected by a group comprised of mostly men. It felt as if I was an equal. Incredible. *Is this how men feel all the time?* The meeting concluded and everyone thanked me for my time. I left the room never feeling so appreciated in my life.

The male privilege snowball never stopped rolling regardless of where I was. At restaurants, if I was with a group of women, I would be addressed first. The host would ask me how many were in the party or where we would like to sit. The server would ask me how the food was, and the manager would look to me when inquiring if we were satisfied with our visit. Even if a woman I was with paid for the meal, the server would hand the bill back to me after running the payment. "Thank you, sir. Have a good night." When entering a store to buy a bottle of wine after dinner, the clerk would only make eye contact with me, not my female friends. People on the street would move out of my way when we walked to my car afterward. I had stepped into an alternate reality, one that felt odd and kind of gross.

After a year or so of this seemingly unwarranted respect, the superiority sadly found its way to my head. I was newly single, out in downtown Austin one night at a bar with a group of friends. As we drank our beers and chatted, a new girl that I had my sights set on texted me that she was at a nightclub only a few miles away. I knew it was too far to walk, so I said goodbye to my friends and proceeded to call a Lyft. My friends were not interested in helping me get laid, and I don't blame them. As I stood outside the bar, drunk and eager, I noticed a car across the street with a lit-up pink Lyft sign. It was clearly not my ride, but I didn't care. I proceeded to walk toward the car anyway. "Jasmine?" the driver asked as I approached the window. I responded with a quick, "Yep," and casually got in.

About half a mile into the drive, the driver's phone rang. He picked up through the car's Bluetooth, and sure enough, it was Jasmine. She began questioning why her app was showing that she had been picked up when she was still waiting at the bar for him to arrive. The driver had a hard time understanding her and eventually ended the call after she asked him to cancel the ride. I knew I had to come up with something. "Sorry man, my girlfriend obviously forgot that she had ordered the ride for me. She was pretty drunk when I left." We laughed together. Clearly it wasn't me, a man, who was at fault, it was my silly drunk girlfriend. *Women can be so daft sometimes.* His reaction assured me that my man card had momentarily secured my position in the situation. Shortly after our laughter abated, Jasmine called for a second time. This call was much less calm, and as she screamed at the driver, I promptly exited the vehicle and ran the last 0.7 miles to the nightclub.

I woke up the next morning feeling extremely disappointed in myself. Sure, I had gotten what I wanted, but I had also let women down. I knew that I could easily convince the Lyft driver that there was no way I, the man, was wrong. I had taken advantage of my newfound male privilege, and I was so angry and disappointed with myself. *Jasmine, if you're reading this, I'm sorry. That was a dick move.* After that minor, yet problematic event, I vowed to myself to never act that way again. I even told my friends about it to keep me accountable just in case. They never stopped teasing me, but I deserved it.

My struggle to ensure I remained cognizant of my male privilege, especially after that night, became somewhat endless and exhausting. I felt uncomfortable in both queer spaces and the straight world, and I grew tired of my inability to just be. When I turned to straight people in my life for advice, I was often met with my second least favorite question, "Well, isn't this what you wanted?" They weren't trying to be cruel, it just didn't make sense to them. *How could it?* I had waited my whole life to be a man and now I was one. Surely, the shift of my place in society couldn't be that problematic.

Even my own dad questioned the validity of my feelings. "You're a guy now, just go be a guy," he would say, encouraging me to branch out into the world. He couldn't possibly comprehend the loss of community or the difficulty of assimilating into a new reality. I grew angry with him for insinuating that my years in the queer world were simply a stepping stone before the straight world—a place I mostly didn't like—accepted me. "I don't want to be in the straight world. I want to be with my people. I love my community," I would shoot back, tears pouring down my cheeks. He meant no harm, he just didn't get it. I desperately missed him being able to solve all my life's "problems." It was hopeless, and I was unable to figure out a path forward alone. To top it all off, my discomfort was coated with a neat layer of guilt. I was only in this situation because I had the privilege of passing so well. *You can't have your cake and eat it too, you ungrateful dick.*

Over time, the horrible thoughts of suicide began to creep back in. I was overwhelmed and unable to see the light at the end of the tunnel. I didn't want to be associated with the male privilege afforded to men for no apparent reason, and I was desperate for my community to somehow recognize me again. I constantly wished for a way that I could signal to my community that I was trans without telling the entire world. *Maybe a secret handshake or symbol?*

Realizing that was never going to be possible, I sought out a local transgender support group in an attempt to find solace. I was eager to meet people I could relate to, either over the loss of queer visibility or any of the other painful realities of transition that I was struggling with. The group met weekly and was composed of about ten people, both transgender men and women. The concept was open forum and any topic was fair game. I sat in the circle desperate for connection during the first meeting.

As the topics for discussion were dissected, I quickly realized how mild my experiences were in comparison to others'. *This isn't going to be my forum after all.* It didn't seem fair to bring up my grief of losing visibility in the queer community while others were struggling to pass at all. Some of the group members were actively on hormones and were still barely seeing any progress. Many of them had been disowned by their families while I had a support network that never stopped reminding me how worthy I am. *I'll just be over here drowning in my privilege.* I left the meetings feeling like a total piece of shit. I tried to convince myself that the pain and discomfort was still valid, but all I felt was guilt for my failure to keep things in perspective. Once again, I hated myself for being so selfish and ungrateful. It could clearly be so much worse.

I stopped attending the group and began the search for an individual therapist. It was time to find one I could actually benefit from. I sought out the mental health resources available through my work, doing all I could to ignore my anxieties that my boss would find out and promptly fire me. *They couldn't have an unstable person managing a team.* The stigma surrounding mental health has always been so terribly detrimental to those seeking help. "Is my boss going to find out about this?" I asked during my first call with the program's customer service representative. "No, all of the information you share with us is kept confidential from your employer. We are a third party, so you have nothing to worry about," she kindly assured me. *Phew.* We set up the search parameters—LGBTQ+ therapist within 10 miles of my apartment—and ended the call once the list came through to my email. It was my job to find the right fit. The program would cover eight sessions of therapy at no cost to me. A welcomed change of pace; I was already thousands of dollars in debt on account of my transition.

I began calling through the list, leaving voicemails and waiting for return correspondence. Russell, one of my top choices on account of his welcoming website, called me back within a day of my voicemail. A promising sign that he was the real deal. Timely communication has always been incredibly important to me. I explained to Russell how poorly I had been doing, especially in the last few months. I needed someone to work through some of my anxieties with me. A live sounding board of sorts. "I thought transition was supposed to help, and I didn't anticipate feeling like this," I explained to him, a pained tone in my voice. "Don't worry, we can figure this out together," Russell responded compassionately. I took the earliest appointment he had available and stopped my search for anyone else. He appeared supportive, and I was desperate for help. I couldn't keep on like this.

The day of the appointment, I nervously waited in the room outside his office while I watched other people come and go from their appointments. I flipped through a magazine to calm my fidgety hands, barely able to focus on the content. Turning the pages was my only task. I had to distract myself somehow; there were so many thoughts rushing around in my head. *Would we be able to get to all of my issues? Would Russell actually be able to help me?* I was so fearful that the answer would be no. *What would I do then?* A kind looking man suddenly appeared in the doorway, momentarily interrupting my thoughts.

Russell was as cute as a button. He was about 5'9" and wore a nicely fitted, short-sleeve button-up with dress pants. Male pattern balding had definitely been present on his mother's side, but he undoubtedly rocked it. A horseshoe of ginger hair wrapped proudly around his head, a shiny circle sitting in the middle of it. We sat down across from one another, his soothing voice assuring me that I was in the right place. I noticed his silly socks, covered with donuts, as his pant leg pulled up slightly. "Cute socks," I said to him, eager to break the ice. "Thank you. My boyfriend got them for me," he chuckled back. I had considered Russell might be gay, but it's never safe to assume. I was thankful to know I had been right. Talking with a member of the community was always more comfortable than not, regardless of being constantly misread.

"So, tell me why you are here," he started out. I explained the hell of transition so far, ultimately leading me to a place that didn't feel sustainable. We spoke of my shame and guilt that had ruined any chance of prior therapy being successful. There had been one other therapist after the garbage first experience. I admitted to feeling judged both times, although there was no evidence of that actually being the case with either of them. I then went on to explain my problematic group therapy experience. Russell looked perplexed, inadvertently proving that I was overthinking it. "Your struggle is relative, and you deserve to feel worthy in it," he responded matter-of-factly. The words hit me like a freight train. *He had a point.* I clearly had a lot of work to do, and I regretted not starting therapy sooner.

HOW DO YOU THINK HORMONES AFFECTED ME?

"Physically, you look so much like your male relatives! The more masculine parts of you were only accentuated, and your curves became more structured and triangular. Still got that booty though ;P

Emotionally, you seemed much more level with hormones (though you've told me your anger felt uncontrollable, which I never really experienced). You seemed more secure and confident in yourself and your place in the world. I don't know that this is hormonal as much as it is you achieving this true form of yourself, but it's noteworthy."

Carrie / First Love, Friend / California

"I have a vivid memory of you FaceTiming me right when your voice started to change. I remember thinking how 'you' that you sounded. It's like all of a sudden your voice fit with your energy and soul. I don't think I ever told you this, but I hung up with you and cried. It made me so happy."

Sammi / Friend / California

"You've always been so relentlessly positive—and it seems like testosterone made you deal with some shit you had been avoiding. I know it was really hard for you—but, ultimately, I think you became YOU. Now you seem so confident, happy and grateful."

Smith / Gaggle Friend / Austin

"I noticed that instances where you would have previously cried or been generally upset, you became angry instead. I essentially watched you go through puberty as a young adult and you were forced to deal with all of the shitty things that go along with that, which I'm certain were compounded by still coming to terms with your gender identity."

Matt / Coworker, Friend, Roommate / Austin

"I know when you started the hormones it was very difficult for you. It takes awhile to find the right amount of hormones to take, and I think the highs/lows of emotions were hard for you. It never affected your professional life but I think it did affect your personal life (love life). Relationships are a lot of work to begin with and are 10x more complicated when you are going through trying to find a balance in a tornado of emotions."

Leatriana / Coworker, Friend / Austin

CHAPTER 9

Male Impersonator

Over time, Russell and I made small improvements. He helped me manage my anxieties little by little each week, and although I stopped thinking about suicide, it would be many more years before I truly felt comfortable with everything that had changed. My professional life mostly returned to normal, and "he" and "James" eventually came more naturally to everyone. There was one coworker, a devout Mormon man, who didn't seem on board with my recent life change, but it honestly seemed more uncomfortable for him than for me. He continued to call me "Lauren" and "she" throughout meetings and conference calls, never faltering. Every time he addressed me incorrectly, everyone would look at him with a confused "What the hell, Jeff?" glare. He would sit there as if nothing out of the ordinary had happened. It was bizarre. I considered talking to him or Shirley about it, but ultimately decided against it. From the beginning, I had told the staff that it was their choice whether or not to respect my name and pronoun change, and I felt too uncomfortable going back on that. *The less attention on my transition, the better.*

When Jeff wasn't outing me, my email address was the only outstanding issue at work. I wasn't "allowed" to change my name in the company directory until I had aligned legal documentation, so I was stuck using my laurenbennett@[company].com email address for what felt like an eternity. I would introduce myself to new staff or site visitors as James and then eventually have to share that emails from me would come from a "Lauren." I never explained why and prayed they wouldn't ask. *Humiliating is an understatement.* I eventually grew so sick of the added stressor, I became determined to find some sort of loophole. I wasn't yet prepared to take on the daunting task of updating my legal documentation.

I figured out that other staff were using their nicknames or shortened names in their email addresses, so why couldn't I? Sure, James wasn't a nickname, but I convinced Shirley there simply wasn't a difference. "There are many Kathryns who go by Katie or Matthews who go by Matt," I told her in another one of our many meetings. "Why is this any different? Katie and Matt aren't their legal names," I continued on. Shirley looked at me, unable to come up with an answer. "You have a good point, James," she said with a smile. Days later, james.bennett@[company].com was made available to me and the relief was overwhelming. To top it off, Jeff finally started calling me by my right name and pronouns too. *Maybe the Book of*

Mormon contains some specific guidance on this type of situation? Who knows, but humor sure does help.

Once the name fiasco was sorted, it was mostly up to me to come out. The freedom was truly liberating. Most days felt relatively painless at work after the first year or so, especially after the staff from Santa Barbara stopped visiting following their site shut down. They were the only people who knew me as a twenty-three-year-old lesbian, and I was selfishly relieved when I no longer had to placate their surprise at seeing me as a man for the first time. It felt all too much like the Philippines airport situation, and I was eager to stay as far away as possible from that feeling. I couldn't afford to waste my energy on such useless interactions.

Outside of work, my legal documentation drained any remaining emotional capacity I had. Everything still said Lauren and Female, and I simply couldn't muster up the courage to face the daunting task. My ID worked fine at queer bars, but as was the case with the majority of my life's experiences, things worked very differently in the straight world. The building discomfort eventually filled me with a burning desire to make everything align. Whenever my legal name came up, confusion consistently followed. Men were the only ones who couldn't resist making jokes about it. *Shocker.*

One joyful afternoon at AT&T, I was forced to tell the two male employees my legal name so they could access my account. As "Lauren Bennett" appeared on the screen, one of the men snickered and said, "Interesting spelling of that name for a guy." I laughed it off and responded, "Yeah, not sure what my parents were thinking on that one." My body grew hot and my palms started to sweat. I did all I could to remind myself that neither of them had any idea I was transgender. Thankfully, there was no "F" on the screen next to my name. The interaction could not be over soon enough. *I have to fix this*, rang loudly through my head as I drove home with my new phone. I'd need a new ID to update my AT&T account, along with everywhere else Lauren made an appearance.

The first step was to obtain a court order. I could then use that document to have my name and marker changed on everything, everywhere. Constance's mom recommended a law firm in Austin that was known for helping transgender clients do just that. Their fee was $1200, an unaffordable cost for most. The lawyers would prepare the court petition and set a court date. They had relationships with the judges and knew which days the "good ones" would be working. On January 16, 2017, I excitedly submitted my check and required paperwork to the firm. The package of documents included letters from my top surgery doc, hormone doc, and therapist. On February 9, 2017, I put on my suit and headed to court. One of the good judges was apparently working that day. *What if they were out sick and I got a bad judge? Would my request be denied?* I pushed down my fears as we entered the building, sweat soaking through my shirt.

Surprisingly, the appointment was quick and painless. The judge was kind and asked me the standard questions that would be asked of anyone changing their name. "Are you changing your name to avoid credit card debt or for criminal purposes?" Etc. Etc. "No, I'm changing my name so I can live more comfortably in society." Ironically, the gender marker was less relevant. I felt relieved when she responded with respect and understanding. We were still in Texas, after all. The judge signed the petition, I had ten copies made, and I was off to the DMV shaking with excitement. For the first time in my life, I had a piece of paper with "James" and "Male" on it. *Hell yes.*

Unfortunately, my visit to the DMV did not go as smoothly as the courthouse. After handing my documentation and court order to the clerk, his face grew increasingly perplexed. *Fuck.* I fumbled to explain what all of it meant. After he garnered an inkling of understanding, he informed me of the bad news. As I wasn't yet a citizen, my state and federal documentation could not be misaligned. If he were to update my driver's license, my state ID wouldn't match my federal ID. That was a huge no-no as immigration still had no idea who James Bennett was. My heart dropped. The clerk saw the desperation in my eyes, tears starting to well in the corners. I had waited so long for this moment. He paused, gave me a reassuring look, and then began processing my paperwork. He wasn't going to be the one to ruin this day. He took my picture, I thanked him profusely, and I was soon on my merry way with my temporary license. My driver's license was set to arrive in the mail a few weeks later. I almost screamed with relief. *One step further away from the discomfort.*

After my new license card arrived, a majority of my day-to-day anxieties were immediately erased. Showing my ID was exciting and validating rather than distressing and nerve-racking. I no longer had to brace myself for questions or pointless comments about my name. There was also a big

"M" where the "F" used to be, which made my soul smile. Life suddenly became a little happier. I quickly set out to change my name on every piece of documentation I could think of.

There was, at the time, no option for "name change due to gender transition," but married people had unknowingly already paved the way. I used the same path women did when they changed their last name to their husband's, but instead of a marriage certificate, I provided my Texas court order coupled with a brief petition. I will never forget the first few times I had to face the blatant "He used to be a woman??" stares from groups of bank employees huddled in corners, looking over at me. I barreled through the discomfort in a matter of months and, slowly but surely, every single one of my bank cards, my social security card, and my college records said James Bradley Bennett. Obtaining my revised diploma was the most complicated task of them all as I still owed my college $79 for a rented book I never returned. They finally got me seven years later. *Good work, UCSB.*

After the intense round of updates, the only remaining hiccup was international travel, and boy, was it a big one. My family and I were still Australian citizens after roughly fifteen years in the States, so we required both our Australian passports and green cards to travel overseas. My documents worked for a trip to England at the end of 2015 (the one the doctor fumbled the letter for), but did not fare so well a few months later. I no longer looked like a Lauren Danielle or female teenager in any capacity. My favorite incident occurred in March of 2016, about nine months into my transition.

Upon arriving at the customs desk in Mexico, Constance and I handed the agent both of our passports. I watched nervously as the agent opened mine up first. She paused briefly and then began asking Constance questions about our travel plans instead of me. *Shit. She thinks that my passport photo is Constance.* We looked nothing alike, but Constance looked more like an eighteen-year-old me than I did. I quickly grew sick to my stomach. I did not want to be a transgender person stuck in Mexico customs. That wasn't safe no matter what country we were in. Constance flawlessly answered the questions and extended her hand when the agent passed her back my passport. Her actual passport was up next. *Uh oh.* The look on the agent's face would have been comical if I wasn't so worried about what was going to happen next. I pictured two large men storming over and arresting me on the spot. Instead, the agent shut Constance's passport after realizing her mistake and handed it back to me. In order to avoid exposing her error in identification, she just let us go. I couldn't believe it. We busted ass out of the airport feeling thankful that the situation ended the way it did. I drank far too many margaritas that night in celebration.

After relaxing for a few days in Mexico, Constance and I flew back to the US. Upon arriving at the US custom's desk, I was faced with another, slightly more problematic interaction. Constance watched helplessly from the line. We had gone up separately this time on purpose. As the agent looked over my passport and green card, he grew more and more perplexed. "Are you going through some kind of surgery or something?"

he asked me, drowning in his own ignorance. *WHAT?* I figured this wasn't the time to educate the man, especially if I wanted to get back into the country. I begrudgingly responded, "Yes." He handed me back my documentation and we were on our way after he seamlessly scanned through Constance's documents. I was happy to be home, but felt disheartened by the agent's complete lack of understanding. The interaction still stands as the most absurd way anyone has ever asked me if I am transgender. Did their training not cover the possibility that they might encounter a transgender person? *We like to travel too, you know.*

In August of 2017, I finally applied for US citizenship. I was sick of the discomfort and my green card was soon to expire. I either had to renew it or apply for citizenship, and it made no sense to do the former. I had to move toward James and away from Lauren. Per the advice of another lawyer friend, I applied for citizenship using my old information, as James had not yet broken into the world of federal documentation. There was an option on the Application for Naturalization that allowed for a request for name change, and although it clearly wasn't for transgender people, the lawyer suggested it didn't matter. I excitedly filled in the little squares with "James Bradley Bennett," opting to deal with the gender marker later. I apprehensively submitted my application with my fingers crossed. My biometrics appointment, the first step of naturalization, was scheduled shortly after. I was terribly nervous, yet overwhelmingly excited. With each hurdle I overcame, I was one step closer to the end of the documentation fiasco.

Upon entering the building in October of 2017, I handed over my documentation to the front desk agent. The gentlemen looked confused, but ushered me to the waiting area anyway. I wanted to explain up front, "Hey, I'm transgender so that's why my documents don't match," but had learned by then that it was easier to let people figure it out on their own. On a good day, I wouldn't have to explain myself at all. "Lauren Bennett," the next agent said as he called me up for my appointment. As expected, the agent grew confused as he reviewed my documentation. *This wasn't going to be one of the good days.* I had no choice but to explain why my documentation looked nothing like me. Both my green card and passport photos were at least eight years old. The man appeared to understand my explanation and proceeded to take my fingerprints.

Shortly after, the man had to make a gender selection on the computer. This is where he hit a significant mental roadblock. He expressed uncertainty as he scrolled back and forth over the options, pausing every few seconds. I stood up to help him, as he clearly needed it. As I looked over his shoulder, I was shocked by what I saw. The standard options of "Male" and "Female" were followed by "Male Impersonator" and "Female Transvestite." *I AM NOT MAKING THIS SHIT UP.* He hovered the mouse over the latter of the two options. I became increasingly more and more uncomfortable. There was no way in hell I was going to let this man choose either of those. I'm pretty sure they aren't even recognized gender identities. He looked up at me and said, "Male impersonator, right?" *Uhm, no.*

I looked over the options again. There was no "Transgender" selection to be found. I showed him my court order and bluntly said to him, "Just choose male. That is what I am." He indifferently responded, "Okay," and made the selection. *Thank God.* I was not about to navigate the rest of the naturalization process as a "Male Impersonator." I don't even know what that means. We finished the appointment, and before I left, I took the time to fill out a detailed customer comment card. "This isn't the 1970s," I wrote. I suggested that they educate their staff and update their gender options to align with the current decade. I beat myself up the entire drive back to work. *You should have been more prepared. You already know that the world isn't set up for people like you.* There would be many more years of bullshit before I finally got it all sorted.

CHAPTER 10

Dirty Jers'

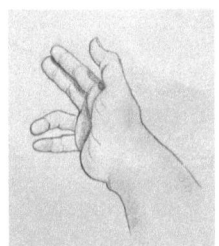

Amid the existing hurdles of 2017, I chose to pursue another. The decision to pursue bottom surgery had less to do with feeling "complete" and more to do with resolving my public bathroom anxiety. I was passing enough to enter the men's room without concern, but sitting down to urinate continued to cause more stress than anything else I have experienced. There were typically only one or two stalls, seats covered in urine, and occasionally, men would enter one and not lock it. I lost count of the number of times I pushed open a door only to hit another man in the back. *Great, more urine on the seat.*

When I did make it into a stall, I enjoyed only a small rush of relief before the next anxiety wave would hit. I worried constantly that the other men in the space would find it weird that I was sitting or somehow notice that my stream of urine sounded noticeably different. *If I sound like their wife peeing, will they know that I'm a biological woman?* My dad did his best to convince me that other men would never notice any of these things, but it still made me sick with anxiety every single time. The fear was rooted in my concern of being "found out." Bathrooms are not typically safe for transgender people, and I wanted no part of that outcome.

When my employer added "Gender reassignment surgeries up to $75,000" to our insurance coverage that year, I nearly jumped with joy. The surgeries could range upward of $30,000 and there was no way I was going to have that kind of money any time soon. I still hadn't made a dent in the $7000 debt from my top surgery only two years prior. The prospect of financial assistance for this massive undertaking made obtaining the surgery seem possible. I had looked in the past, but never too seriously. Bottom surgery had always seemed too far off to be even remotely attainable.

There were two surgeries to consider: Metoidioplasty (Meta) or Phalloplasty (Phallo). The vagina can stay or go regardless. Testicular implants can be added if desired. Meta, meaning "toward male genitalia," builds a phallus of sorts, using what naturally happens to the clitoris when a biological woman takes testosterone. With the introduction of male hormones, the clitoris grows, varying in length across individuals. The surgery then lengthens the urethra along the bottom of this growth, with the aim of allowing the patient to pee standing up. Phallo, a much more invasive surgery, takes tissue from the forearm, thigh, or back and creates a more typical looking phallus that should function similarly to that of a cisgender male. The only caveat is the lack of erectile function. There are medical device options available, but my research didn't prove all that helpful on that part. I needed professional input to make a decision. There were two doctors that seemed popular in the community, one in Austin and one in San Francisco. Considering I was already in Austin, there was no decision to make. Limiting travel time and expense in any capacity would be helpful. I set an appointment and anxiously waited. This was a much more intense decision than having my breasts removed. Bottom surgery had the potential to negatively affect my life in extreme ways, most specifically my sex life. I was terrified.

The day of the appointment, I laid on the uncomfortable half bed, half chair while the doctor and his nurse prodded at my genitals. *Do they think I'm disgusting? Are they questioning why I'd want to do this to my body?* They hadn't said or done anything of the sort to suggest it, but I was shamefully embarrassed nonetheless. When the physical exam finally ended, I was relieved to pull my underwear back up. The doctor seemed pleased with what he had to work with, temporarily offsetting my shame. I cracked a brief smile. My questions were up next. I had a lengthy pros and cons list for each surgery, with concerns noted next to a majority of the bullet points. The doctor's responses confirmed that my research had proven helpful. I was allegedly prepared for what to expect.

After the Q&A session, the doctor opened a drawer and handed me a gumby-like medical device. The first of two options. I bent it back and forth while we talked about possible complications. The other option, a pump of sorts, sat untouched on the counter. Considering my career in medical devices, my questions were a little more specific than most. I had spent years working with adverse event data at work, investigating everything that can go wrong with different products. There is no such thing as a permanent medical device, and I couldn't stand the thought of going through multiple bouts of revision surgery decades in the future. I was set on eventually becoming a CEO, and there would be no time for lengthy absences. Phallo seemed less appealing the more our discussion progressed.

As the office doors closed behind me, I called my parents immediately to process. I never in my life thought I would be discussing my genitals with them, but I didn't have a choice. I certainly did not want to make this weighty decision by myself, and Constance and I had broken up months ago. We were still desperately in love, but our issues had become impossible to ignore. Our communication styles were incompatible and our relationship fell apart more dramatically the further into my transition I went. Neither of us could stand the yelling or constant tension, so the love affair had to end.

My parents listened as I intently explained my options. My body wouldn't stop shaking. We discussed the lengthy recovery process that would inevitably follow Phallo and the potentially disastrous scarring that could result from the donor sites. I explained the flimsiness of the medical devices used to give the appearance and minimal functionality of male genitalia. Implanting any device like that would also increase the likelihood of revision surgeries in the future if they malfunctioned. My main goal was to be able to urinate standing up, and considering that was an expected outcome of both surgeries, the decision essentially made itself. I opted for the less invasive Meta surgery with hopes that the outcome would prove advantageous for navigating the men's restroom and ultimately require less recovery time. I had a life to live, and I couldn't be out of commission for months. I thanked my parents profusely and called the doctor's office to schedule surgery. August 3, 2017. *Deep breaths.*

Leading up to the surgery, a sense of grief that I never expected overtook me. I was two years into my transition, and this was the first time I genuinely processed the loss of Lauren, my former self. Each physical change that had taken place prior did not seem nearly as final as this one. I had wanted my breasts gone since the moment they started to develop, so there was only excitement (and some fear) during the time leading up to top surgery. Bottom surgery felt like the final physical step toward saying goodbye to Lauren for good. The emotional pain was excruciating, and I met with Russell often to work through it.

"I just feel like I'm telling Lauren she wasn't good enough," I said as I sat across from him bawling my eyes out. "I want to get closer to male genitalia, but I didn't expect to feel like the person closest to me was dying on the way there. These changes are permanent, and there is no turning back."

Russell looked at me reassuringly like he always did. "Why don't you reframe it as being thankful for Lauren? You don't have to focus on her leaving."

I looked around hopelessly, depleted of all energy. "Easier said than done," I responded, "but I will do my best to think about it differently." I spent the next few weeks doing all I could to work through it.

Thankfully, when the time came, the surgery itself served as a sufficient distraction from any lingering grief. My dad also flew out to spend the first week of recovery with me, alleviating the pain that remained. He was there to drop me off and wheel me out. As soon as I came to, he grabbed my hand and relayed what the doctor had said. Everything had gone well and we were free to head out once the anesthesia effects wore off. I smiled as I laid my head down on the starchy pillow. *One step closer to relief.* I jumped on Instagram to share the news, posting a selfie of me in a hospital bed cryptically captioned, "All good! :)" I hadn't planned on telling my entire network of friends and acquaintances, but drugs do crazy things.

After being discharged, I spent the next week "taking it easy," at the request of my doctor, and ordering my dad around. He brought me tacos in bed, sat through any movie I requested, and laughed when I told him he wasn't the president of the United States. I was not impressed when he was momentarily distracted from taking care of me due to a work call. *Sorry, Dad.* The downside of the recovery was heavy bandaging and an extremely uncomfortable suprapubic catheter. The catheter was attached to a bag that I had to carry around everywhere with me. The insertion site became increasingly red and painful with each passing day, rubbing every time I moved.

A few days in, I finally felt as if I could go number two. The constipation on account of the pain meds was no match for the amount of prune juice I had consumed. I headed into the bathroom while my dad and I laughed from either side of the closed door. Through the pushing, my bandages shimmied loose and my newly constructed genitals were exposed to me for the first time. I looked down in absolute horror, my laughter quickly abating. *WHAT THE FUCK DID YOU DO?* The reality of what I had done hit me like a freight train. Everything looked swollen and disgusting, and I was mortified. I covered myself back up and hobbled into my bedroom across the hall. My dad asked if I was okay, although he was already well aware of the answer.

I paced back and forth in my bedroom while my thoughts spiraled out of control. *What if it always looks like this? Is anyone ever going to have sex with me again? Why didn't I just leave my body alone?* Over and over, down and down. Dad eventually asked again if I was okay. I came out of the room and hugged him as tight as I could muster. We stood there for what felt like an eternity, and I vividly remember how cold the floor felt on my bare feet. Dad asked what was wrong, but I couldn't speak through the tears. They just kept coming. He waited patiently, and I eventually calmed down enough to form words. "The bandage fell off, and I don't like how it looks," I said. He didn't need the specifics to understand. He assured me that everything was going to be fine, just like he always did. He reminded me that I was still very swollen, how soon after surgery it was, and how it would naturally take a while to get used to the way things looked. Dad would eventually be proven right, but I didn't believe him that day.

The good ol' catheter bag

After my dad departed, I was left anxiously waiting to see if my surgery had been successful. The nurse had switched me over from the clunky catheter bag to a nifty valve apparatus that taped to my thigh. It was slightly more comfortable and gave me a nice preview of what it would be like to pee standing up. When I had to urinate, I would pull off the tape, aim the apparatus over the toilet bowl, push the side lever forward, and the urine would flow out. When the bladder emptied, there would be a strange pulling sensation deep inside me, and I would know to push the lever back again to close the valve. I had to keep the catheter in for at least three weeks before I was to try urinating without it. If all went well, the catheter would come out at week four. It was all terribly lonely. On the outside, I looked "normal," but underneath my clothes sat an irritated catheter site, surgical tape pulling at my thigh hair, and a valve that I had to open and close to urinate. I struggled in silent, isolating pain.

At the three-week mark, the doctor instructed me to stand over the toilet and just "try to pee." The fear was nauseating; I was unsure if the flow would be painful when it started. Everything had laid dormant since surgery, circumnavigated by the catheter's function. I stood over the toilet shaking. My left hand rested on the top of the tank while I mustered up the courage to face what was about to happen. I worried incessantly how the impending sensation would feel as I pushed in the way that my muscle memory encouraged. At first, the stream appeared to come out of the correct spot, but then something jolting happened. I felt a well of urine pooling somewhere else, in unison with a slight tingling sensation, and then a second stream began. This was all new, but I was sure urine wasn't supposed to be coming out of two places. Panic ensued. *Something can't be right.* The loneliness sliced through me. I stood over the toilet, blank. *What the fuck am I doing with my life?* An eternity passed before I mustered up the strength to call my doctor.

The doctor's tone surprised me. He nonchalantly informed me that I most likely had a "fistula," a channel the body forms from one organ to another. I had seen the word during the signing of the consent forms, but I hadn't actually considered it might happen to me. My concerns were with aesthetics and sensation, not weird unexpected streams of urine. There was no way I could comfortably pee standing up in a public men's room like this. Disappointed was an understatement. All of the pain, loneliness, and anxiety were for nothing. The doctor encouraged me to keep the catheter in for a few more weeks. The fistula could supposedly heal itself over time, but I was not convinced. I was angry and mentally checked out.

I kept the catheter in for as long as I could bear. The wound was red and angry, and each movement continued to pull the tube against the most irritated parts. The pain eventually won, so I called the doctor to schedule the removal. A few hours later, we met at his office in between two of his scheduled surgeries. We talked briefly, but I couldn't focus on anything. I just wanted the ordeal to be over. I pulled down my pants, he cut the tube, and with one big tug, the rest of the catheter came out of my bladder. I could feel the tubing uncoil inside me as he yanked it out. Urine went everywhere. *Disgusting, just like me.* I thanked him and scurried out of the room, defeated and alone.

A month later, I had somewhat "recovered" from the mind fuck of the failed first surgery and was ready for something new. I was borderline floundering, avoiding any environment that wasn't comfortable, and my uneasiness around men was still unbearably obvious. In unison, my career had hit somewhat of a wall. The department director was threatened by my ambition, and unless one of the managers randomly got hit by a bus, I was not going to get promoted anytime soon. I needed a change.

My romantic life, albeit immensely enjoyable, was also not in a place that made staying in Austin the obvious choice. A few months after Constance and I had finally called it quits, I found the courage to face the daunting task of finding partnership again. I was still desperately unsure of my new self and meeting women had somehow become a foreign challenge. I had no idea where to start. *Do I seek out straight women and tell them I'm trans or do I seek out queer women in the spaces where my true identity is no longer apparent?* I ultimately settled on the latter. I didn't spend enough time in straight spaces, and the thought of having to come out to a straight woman as transgender sounded terrible. At least in queer spaces it would be less of a surprise. My only hurdle would be getting women to notice me there. I had no idea how it would go after that disclosure. *Will women still be attracted to me in this form? Am I still queer enough?*

Eventually, a woman from my friend group showed enough interest in me that even my insecurities couldn't talk me out of responding to her pursuit. Julia had been part of the Gaggle for some time and had never known me as Lauren. I didn't understand why she was attracted to me, but I also couldn't continue to avoid being with women on account of my diminished self-worth. She had subtly set her sights on me months prior, when Constance and I were still together. We had met through one of the Gaggle brunches, flirting incessantly after she accidentally dropped part of her cinnamon roll in my iced coffee. I was captivated by her. She was quirky and gorgeous in a way that she was unaware of. Her energy was electric and her curly brown hair served as a constant distraction when we were around one another. Some time after the breakup, Julia eventually texted me and asked me to join her at a karaoke party. I hated karaoke, but I hated the idea of losing the opportunity to be with her even more. I had been thinking about her for weeks, and I had to take this leap of faith. I hated how scared I was. As Lauren, I would have jumped at the opportunity to be with this woman right away, and suddenly, I was questioning why a woman wanted to be with me at all.

After a duo performance of 50 Cent's "How We Do" (would not recommend for a karaoke selection), we finally took our flirting to the next level. Julia suggested that we go swimming just the two of us at my apartment pool, and I was terrified. I pushed my fears as deep down as they would go and agreed to her request. We arrived back at my place, hopped over the chained gate, and got into the pool as quietly as we could. The pool was clearly closed, but the opportunity was far too tempting. We waded in the water, locking eyes every few seconds. I was overwhelmingly nervous, but as the conversation flowed,

I felt more confident to move closer. She wrapped her legs around me and we began kissing. The questions of inadequacy ravaged my mind. Why can't I be taller so I can hold her higher out of the water? Is she going to think my body looks weird, or big and gross, if she sees me naked? Will she be disgusted by my excess body hair and terrible bacne? I forced myself to embrace the moment.

The next morning, I woke up feeling like a new person. My first romantic experience as James had thankfully been a good one, and I was incredibly grateful. Julia was understanding and validating, and she unknowingly helped me realize that I should start to let go of my fears. *I am still worthy of affection even though I am transgender*, rang through my head for the first time. Maybe there would be fewer women who wanted James over Lauren, but after that night, I felt reassured that I wasn't destined to be alone forever. I was thankful for the momentary reprieve from the negative narrative I had spun in my head. My insecurities with my new body still remained, but my confidence in James as a person had begun its slow ascent.

Over the next six months, Julia and I continued to enjoy one another. I adored her lust for life, and she continuously challenged me to face new social experiences. We spent a lot of time together, but never committed to monogamy. I had a lot of work to do on myself, and neither of us were interested in settling down with one person. We both appreciated the freedom to explore who we were in relation to multiple partners. (Disclaimer: This is not what polyamory looks like for everyone.) Outside of Julia, I pursued a few in-person connections and eventually branched out into the world of queer dating apps as well. I was able to include my transgender identity on my profile, and the anxiety of coming out in person was removed as a result. After a few unsuccessful dates from the online pool, I came across a woman's profile that spiked my interest. Shanay had a girl next door type vibe, coupled with beautiful curly hair, an obvious weakness of mine. She had hearted my profile, and I was given the option of doing the same. If I did, we'd be granted the opportunity to message one another. I hit the cute little red heart and we were soon texting back and forth, scheduling our first date. Shanay lived about an hour and a half south of me and was the manager of a primate sanctuary. Pretty fucking cool. She typically spent her free time in Austin since the dating scene and nightlife near her were generally lackluster, as they were in most of the small towns in Texas.

Days later, I was sitting across from Shanay, sporting a scabbed lip and bandages on three of my four appendages from a bike accident a few days prior. I came down a hill too fast and my face momentarily met the pavement. *Testosterone is crazy.* I concluded she would either think I was completely gross or a total badass. Based on our interaction, I somehow walked away unsure how she felt about me at all. She was quiet and only asked me one question during our entire date. "Do you really cycle all those miles for fun?" I laughed in response. "Yes, yes I do. I love biking more than anything, except for corgis and my parents," I said back. She smiled, clearly perplexed why someone would enjoy such a thing. We spent the rest of our time together in a one-sided Q&A. I've always loved getting to know people, and I had never met anyone who worked at a primate sanctuary. She seemed happy to answer my questions, so we talked until I had nothing left to ask. We hugged goodbye, and I drove off thinking we'd probably never see each other again. There simply wasn't much chemistry there.

The following week, Shanay reached out to let me know she'd be back in town that weekend. I was surprised to hear from her, albeit not opposed to the idea of a second date. Regardless of our lack of conversation, she was pretty and I definitely didn't mind the idea of sitting across from her for a few more hours. We agreed to meet up that Thursday, choosing to attend a film screening downtown. The night was ultimately uneventful and doubled down on my certainty that we weren't going to be together. When the film ended, we hopped in my car, and I began to drive in the direction of her Airbnb. Out of the blue, she asked, "Which way is your apartment?" *Does this girl really want to pursue this?* I was shocked. "The opposite way of your Airbnb," I said coyly. "Do you want to come over for a drink?" My confidence was slightly up from Julia, and if this wasn't an effort to spend more time together, I didn't know what was. "Sure!" she responded eagerly. My heart dropped a tad. I was excited at the new prospect of being intimate, yet that meant I had to face my problematic body insecurities once again. She had never been with a transman, and although Julia had made me feel desired, I was convinced Shanay would feel differently. *She will regret this as soon as we are naked together,* my mind cruelly persuaded me.

Surprisingly, quite the opposite happened. After about thirty minutes of strained conversation, we moved to my bedroom and began kissing. The physical chemistry we shared was nothing short of mind-blowing. I had never felt anything like it and couldn't make sense of where on earth it came from. Our bodies seemed to fit together in a way I'd never experienced, and Shanay was eager to learn the nuances of my trans body. I was seemingly perfect to her, and over the next few months, we were both consumed with the desire to keep exploring what we had found. She taught me that my body was valuable on account of my transition, and I couldn't get enough. I was able to be completely uninhibited for the first time since becoming James, and I felt permission to finally embrace my masculinity in a way that I had always wanted. I enjoyed using the prosthetics far more than I ever had, and our connection felt like a drug to me. It was obvious that Shanay was here for the long haul. It didn't matter that we sometimes struggled to make conversation at dinner.

By September 2017, a few months into my relationship with Shanay, I had to take a bold career leap for my future regardless of our status. I couldn't stay in Austin no matter how hot my intimate life was. I made my LinkedIn visible to recruiters, and to my surprise, within weeks I was stacked with phone interviews for multiple different medical devices companies on the East Coast. I had never pictured myself there, but nothing was off the table at this point. I owed it to myself to try. I had to face my fears of assimilation head on if I was ever going to get over them. Before I could stop myself, I was on a plane to New

Jersey, suit in hand, for my first in-person interview. I'd already had three phone interviews and the company seemed eager.

Following a successful day with my prospective new team, I went to dinner with an acquaintance whom I'd met through Jamie. John had relocated from Austin to New Jersey a year prior to work for the company I had just interviewed with. I was thankful for the connection, albeit nervous for how the evening would go. Comically, I was more anxious in anticipation of the dinner than I had been about the job interview. John was a cisgender, straight man, and I worried that I wouldn't know how to act around him. He didn't know I was transgender, and I convinced myself he'd think my behavior was strange.

We met at his house, and to my surprise, John had a jovial, personable demeanor that made me feel comfortable. There wasn't a remote inkling of the overt masculinity or machismo that I couldn't stand. He and I enjoyed a nice dinner at a local restaurant, moving down to their basement bar afterward for drinks. As I sat there with my beer, I realized that this was the first time in my life that I was at a straight bar with another man. John and I were just two dudes drinking our beers and nobody knew otherwise. I felt a shiver of pride tingle through my body as I looked around at my new environment. I was moving my career forward while simultaneously challenging myself in a way that I hadn't ever done before. *You've got balls, James*, I chuckled to myself.

After a few beers, I suggested to John that we find a billiards bar to play some pool. I am good at pool and any attempt to find an inkling of my innate confidence seemed like a logical move. I wanted to keep feeling good about this milestone of an evening. The bartender recommended a local dive bar that was a few blocks away. As we gathered our things, she preemptively warned us, "Watch out for the Spanish pool sharks." John and I laughed in response. "What do you mean?" I asked. The bartender went on to explain how a couple of men would show up a little later in the evening, unsuspectingly, and completely annihilate the table. We thanked her for the advice and were on our way. We found the bar and after we got our drinks, I started clearing the table. My confidence soared as I continued to pocket balls.

After some time, the Spanish pool sharks inevitably showed up. I was on my game, so I suggested that they play John and me in doubles. John was terrible at pool, self-proclaimed, so it was my job to carry our team to victory. We lost in the end, but I was immensely proud of myself for playing at all. As we were leaving, one of the Spanish pool sharks extended his hand to me. "You're good, man," he said as he shook my hand with conviction. I thanked him and internally patted myself on the back for a triumphant evening. My self-confidence had persevered over my self-doubt. *Now I just have to translate this confidence to my potential new life*, I told myself as I drifted off to sleep that night.

I ended up getting the job, and in January of 2018, I packed up my life in Austin and relocated to New Jersey. Shanay stayed behind, and although she'd visit often for the first six months, I was destined for an isolating reality. Shifting my entire life to

Jersey wasn't going to be as seamless as playing a good game of pool. The moment I stepped off the plane, nobody would know that I was born anything other than male. At work, I would just be James, the new supervisor from Austin. Human Resources knew, but that was a matter of necessity. I had no choice but to explain my mismatching documentation for my background check to clear. I worried incessantly what my new coworkers, outside of John, would think of me as James. I didn't even truly know who he was yet, at least not without reference to my prior self.

The night before my first day, I sat in my hotel room, terrified and alone, wondering what the fuck I was doing with my life. Bailee had to fly out a week later due to the cold weather, and I still had my catheter in from a failed fistula revision a few weeks prior. I had crammed in the desperate surgery before departing Austin in an attempt to take advantage of my reached out of pocket maximum. The fistula had persevered per my last pee check before boarding the plane. I once again had to leave the catheter in for a few weeks to see if my body magically reversed its course. Not an ideal situation, but at least I could pee standing up while wearing it.

My chest was tight and I barely slept. I tossed and turned all night, worrying about the fistula and whether or not I would be able to fit in at my new job. I woke up hours before my alarm and spent far too much time overanalyzing my outfit in the mirror. *Would they notice how small my feet were or that I had no bulge in my work pants? Were my clothes too tight overall? Was the catheter visible? Fuck.*

CHAPTER 11

A Botched Goodbye

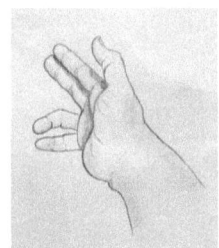

The first week of my new job was as rough as I had imagined it would be. It was hard to be excited about the amazing role I had just landed when I couldn't stop obsessing over what everyone thought of me. As usual, the women didn't seem the least bit interested, and the men all seemingly towered over me. A few looked like they had stepped straight out of a magazine catalog. To make matters worse, I was one of the only non-engineers in a division full of them. Everyone seemed smarter, more attractive, and light years more confident than I could ever be. I grew painstakingly critical of each social interaction and found myself mostly powerless over my resulting anxiety. I had never felt so sick.

The immense discomfort was compounded by my inability to find a doctor in Jersey that would take out my catheter. As expected, the extra time with the catheter hadn't forced my body to heal itself. It was time to call it quits and get the damn thing out. Every doctor's office I called responded with overwhelming confusion. They could not understand why I had a suprapubic catheter and sharing details of my surgery only added to the discomfort for both parties. I eventually resorted to calling my doctor back home to explain my dilemma. We discussed me flying back, but I didn't have the money or the time for that. I had just started the new job and my boss didn't have any idea about my surgery or my catheter. She probably still thought I was a cis man.

After going back and forth for ten minutes, it hit me. *I can take this thing out.* I had seen the doctor do it only six months prior and it didn't look that hard. I proposed my idea to him, and although he was hesitant, he gave in on account of my desperation. He explained the specifics, and I headed back to John's house to get to work. He had graciously invited me to stay with him until I found a place. John not only didn't know about the catheter, I still hadn't told him that I was trans. It hadn't come up during our pool night, and now was certainly not the time.

After a brief chat about our workdays, I headed upstairs to find something sharp. My search proved unsuccessful, so I improvised. "I need to cut this tag off my new shirt," I told him after coming back downstairs. John opened up the kitchen drawer and handed me a pair of scissors. I retreated to the guest bathroom. I figured it would be best to do it in the bathtub; less messy. I would then take a shower and the entire thing would appear totally normal to John.

After a few minutes of digging around, I found the stitch that held the tube to my skin and snipped it. Now came the scary part. *What if I pull this thing and it gets stuck on something inside of me?* The deafening loneliness started to creep back in again, accompanied by the all too familiar theme of, *What the fuck am I doing with my life?* I counted down, *3, 2, 1* and pulled on the tube. In one fell swoop, the catheter came out. I showered myself off and hid the catheter deep inside the trash can under everything else. I didn't want poor John to find it; that would be an entirely ridiculous way to come out. I got dressed and trotted back downstairs for dinner. *Everything was fine and nothing had happened.*

I headed to work the next day feeling slightly relieved, yet still unsure how to navigate any part of my new environment. I desperately wanted to tell everyone, including John, why I seemed a bit different, but I simply didn't know how. This was all new to me and there was no quick fix. In Austin, people had seen my transition first hand, and I assumed that new staff members were eventually told by the older ones. I imagined the conversation would start with, "Want to know something crazy about James?" and from there shock would surely ensue. In Jersey, there was no potential for rumors about my trans identity, and ironically, I found myself missing that. I feared that if I began to tell people myself, I would somehow make them uncomfortable. With society's focus on transgender people's genitals, I was convinced that coming out would somehow force these strangers to think about what was in my pants. Off to HR they would go, reporting the new pervert supervisor in Post Market Surveillance for his inappropriate workplace behavior. *My nightmare.* The all too familiar feeling of wanting to disappear quickly came back again.

One day in the break room, I began chatting with a male coworker whom I knew to be gay. Kevin was openly out in the office, and I was eager to connect with him. It didn't matter that he thought I was cisgender. I was relieved to finally be around someone from my community, although the welcomed comfort was unfortunately short-lived. Minutes into our conversation, I quickly realized that Kevin had perceived me to be gay as well. I had spent enough time immersed in the queer community to know the signals and conversation topics. I panicked and quickly weaved "my girlfriend" into the conversation. He looked confused, but I didn't care. I had to rubber stamp that my identity was not what he had perceived. I hadn't gone through all of this to be misread forever.

A week or so later, after hours spent perseverating on the painful interaction, I asked Kevin if he wanted to get dinner. We lived minutes from each other, and I had to set the record straight. *No pun intended.* We set a date a few days out, and I spent the majority of my time in the interim trying to obtain my hormones. The pharmacies in Jersey had refused to "transfer the prescription across state lines" and therefore left me without the proper materials for my weekly shot. I grew panicked at the prospect; I couldn't just miss a dose. *What would happen to my body and mind?* In a desperate attempt at improvisation, I fished a few used syringes I had stored in a milk jug and threw them into a pot of boiling water. Google didn't prove all that helpful in confirming I wasn't going to get a nasty infection, but I had no other choice. The isolation roared loudly as I watched the syringes bob around. I couldn't wait to get to dinner, testosterone coursing through my veins.

My plan was to come out to Kevin and from there, surely be introduced to his queer social circle. I would no longer be alone, and my life in Jersey could begin. *Everything was going to be okay.* I arrived at the restaurant thirty minutes later and found a moment to come out shortly into our conversation. We discussed my life before moving to Jersey, and I nonchalantly referenced how great Austin had been for my transition. I spoke of how there had been many other transgender folks there and what an amazing queer community I had found. Kevin responded with surprise, "Oh, so you are trans?!" I joked with him that I had an inkling he thought I was gay. He admitted to being confused when I initially mentioned having a girlfriend. He reportedly began wondering if I was trans after that.

He told me of how excited he was when he first met me in the office. He had texted another coworker about "this cute new gay guy." He told me of all the people that came up to him and asked if he thought I was gay when I first started. My heart sank. I was relieved to have finally come out to someone in New Jersey, but was disheartened to hear this revelation of how I was perceived. I struggled to understand my new reality.

As a passing man in a queer space, "gay man" was the most obvious choice, but I had no idea why this was happening in the straight world. After dinner, I spent the rest of the night cycling around in my thoughts, desperately trying to figure out a solution.

Conveniently, Shanay's next visit was scheduled the same weekend as my company's upcoming Christmas party. I was hopeful that her presence would help secure my identity to my coworkers. *One step in the right direction.* She hated that sort of thing, but she obliged as she knew what I was struggling with. I set out with optimism, but the event did nothing to assuage my discomfort. Instead of finding any reprieve, I spent the entire time worrying that my coworkers would assume that Shanay was some type of "beard," an effort to conceal my true sexual orientation. *It was all hopeless.* Shanay flew home shortly after, and I continued to struggle for months with the shift in my reality.

Nothing made sense, and I didn't know how to fix it. I had spent twenty-five years in the wrong body, ten of those defaulting to an identity of lesbian that I didn't relate to, and now I was going to spend the rest of my life in the right body while still being misread? *Seriously?* Being read as gay wasn't a bad thing, I just wasn't gay. *I can't do this forever,* began to play on repeat over and over in my head for the second time in my life. To drown it out, I threw myself into my work. I learned the engineering terms as quickly as possible and attempted to display myself as a reliable people manager. I hoped these efforts would help me fit in a little more succinctly, regardless of my confusing identity.

After memorizing what "ductile overload" and "torsional force" were, I set out to improve my physique. I figured if my body looked better, some of my feelings of physical inferiority standing next to my GQ model coworkers would be minorly alleviated. My work had a gym on-site, so I mustered up the confidence to give that a go. Unsurprisingly, I lasted two days before my anxiety got the best of me. I had never set foot in a men's locker room before and was debilitated by not knowing how to navigate this foreign space. I couldn't stand the thought of changing in front of other men, especially the Adonis-like engineers. I didn't want them to see my chest scars and was too self-conscious to face the thought of what they would think of the rest of my body.

On top of that, I had no idea how we were supposed to interact. *Did men talk to each other in the locker room? Are we allowed to make eye contact?* My coworkers often joked about how the VP would walk around naked after getting out of the shower, and I dreaded not knowing what to do if that happened while I was in there. I would have rather disappeared than be stuck in that situation. I resorted to changing in the bathroom stall, shaking with anxiety each time. I had no idea if doing this was "normal," but I couldn't come up with a better solution.

On my second day at the gym, I made it past the changing stage and began working out in an area that typically had fewer people. Not long into my workout, one of the other managers joined me. I gave him the awkward male head nod that I had still not even remotely mastered and attempted to continue focusing on my exercises. After a few painful minutes, I had to give up. I couldn't do it. I was too self-conscious that I would somehow look weak or my workout would be "wrong." The office gym was apparently not an option after all. I grabbed my things and left.

I worried incessantly in meetings, in the cafeteria, and during after-work happy hours that my behavior appeared abnormal. Years of being socialized as a woman had ingrained behaviors in me that I was challenged to undo as a man. I learned to stop tightly crossing my legs and had to remember not to instinctively reach out my arm to connect with people during conversation. I would recoil in panic if I ever forgot, especially when conversing with another man. I barely knew how to act, and my passing body only served as a reason I should have the standard "male" behaviors down pat.

When I used the restroom, I tried desperately to remember the male codes of conduct I had learned. 1) Eye contact is **NEVER** allowed, 2) pass other men as if they don't exist, and 3) don't even think about making conversation. That is a huge no-no. The basic expectation is to get in, get out, and not look at anyone or anything in the process—a stark contrast to the social etiquette in women's restrooms. Women are allowed to chat, pass toilet paper under the stalls, and compliment each other's outfits. I couldn't make sense of this new, seemingly homophobic space I was expected to exist in with ease. The anxiety caused by my audible two streams of urine only served to compound my discomfort.

When I left work during lunch for something simple like a haircut, I would spend the entire time painstakingly analyzing how I was acting. I would sit in the chair, hot and uncomfortable, and watch how the other men held their bodies. I attempted to sit like they did while I studied how they interacted with each other seemingly with ease. *Stop staring, James. You look like a weirdo.* I grew so envious of their ability to connect, yet prayed that they wouldn't try to engage me in conversation. I was too busy focusing on how I was sitting in the stupid chair. The nuances were endless and exhausting. I was far beyond ill equipped to navigate these foreign societal norms.

As I was leaving the shop one day, I attempted to say goodbye to my barber in the way that the other men did. *Maybe this will help me fit in?* I naively thought to myself. A male acquaintance had previously given me lessons when we were drunk one night, and I thought I had adequately learned the basics. As I attempted the first step of moving from our typical handshake to the hand embrace, my barber looked at me, perplexed. *Shit. I screwed this up.* I quickly withdrew my hand. On account of the barber's confused stare, it was clear that I had not yet mastered this foreign male behavior. I didn't even get a chance to try the body embrace part, although I wasn't too upset about that. I could never seem to understand the line between the hand embrace that leads to the body embrace versus the hand embrace that just ends there. It was all so terribly confusing, foreign, and unnatural. As a woman, I just hugged everyone, and suddenly I was unable to even "normally" say goodbye to another man.

When I eventually moved past some of my physical discomfort and mustered up the courage to try and participate in conversation, I had no idea what I was supposed to talk about. Men rarely seemed to connect with one another on any emotional level, and I didn't know how to contribute in any other way. It was always about sports, fishing trips, or in the worst cases, women. A portion of the men I encountered (not all of them) participated in some level of this awful banter, and I found myself constantly disenfranchised by their sexist, derogatory remarks. It seemingly brought them closer to one another to degrade women in groups. I struggled constantly to play off my disinterest in this strange form of bonding. I still hadn't forgiven myself for taking Jasmine's Lyft.

At that same barbershop one afternoon, a woman brought her young son in for a haircut. After they left, the son's barber turned to me and my barber. "Damn, she's fine, isn't she?" Okay, not too bad, acknowledging an attractive woman isn't a crime. But then it turned. My barber, whom I had somewhat liked until this moment, went on to explain why the woman had dyed her hair platinum blonde over her natural brown. "She did her hair like that for the same reason girls do their tits or ass. They want that attention. When I knew her back in the day, her hair was natural." The disgusting spiral continued. "She's still hot now, but man, back in the day." The men beamed at each other. "Her body used to be so tight. It's not the same now, you know, cause she had a kid." I sat there, helpless to conjure up an appropriate response. "Yeah, I prefer brunettes," was the least derogatory comment I could come up with.

During a phone interview a few weeks later, the man with whom I was interviewing answered the phone in place of a secretary. "I guess I'm playing secretary in a mini skirt today," he said when I asked to speak with the hiring manager. He was, in fact, the hiring manager. I held my tongue and said nothing in response. I had no desire to drown in sexism alongside him. The expectation for acknowledgment was strange and uncomfortable. I appreciated not being the target of it, but failed to understand why this behavior was not just acceptable but a point of bonding. I felt relieved when I didn't get the in-person interview.

A few months after the ridiculous phone interaction, I was invited to speak at the global sales meeting for the company I worked for. One afternoon of the three-day event, I accompanied two of the sales representatives as we moved from one workshop to another. There were both 6'5" and most likely ex-college football players. *My nightmare.* As we walked together, they asked what I did for the company. I explained to them that I worked in the "complaints department" and that my team handled all the failure analysis investigations for our products. One of the men smugly responded, "Oh the complaints department? Can you speak to my wife?" The other man erupted in laughter. I smiled, shook my head, and responded that my department didn't handle inquiries of that nature. It was the best response I could come up with while still attempting to blend in.

Before I had time to recover, the other man proceeded to tell us about how his wife couldn't figure out an issue with the Wi-Fi while he was away. From the way he described her, she didn't sound remotely intelligent or capable. I couldn't understand why he was speaking so poorly of the woman he had married. Has he never had a problem with the Wi-Fi? I didn't realize Wi-Fi problems were gender-specific. I left the conversation as soon as we entered the conference room. I clearly wasn't going to bond with these men, and it only served to heighten my anxiety before I had to speak in front of a room of five hundred of them.

These subtle, or not so subtle, interactions were constant, and I never engaged beyond an awkward smile, short sentence, or a chuckle. It was everywhere every day, and I couldn't escape it. Male acquaintances had a barrage of constant sexual innuendos or "jokes" that they told in mixed company. It appeared to be their only form of communication at times—a second language that I never learned. I felt bad for the women they were with in these situations. They had no choice but to laugh awkwardly and shake their heads. *Oh men, you can be sooo intolerable. LOL.* When they weren't making directly offensive remarks, men would talk of their wives as if they were incapable of basic tasks. "Oh yeah, she is a terrible driver" or "Don't let her near the kitchen." I often wondered if these men ever looked in the mirror and asked themselves what made them so great.

I constantly worried that if I didn't participate, I would seem weird or perpetuate the notion that I was gay. On the other hand, I felt like a complete coward for not speaking up. I wished I could stop this behavior, but fear of ostracizing myself remained my priority. I had to protect my well-being, both physically and emotionally. I was barely confident enough just existing, and I couldn't imagine how the sales training would have gone if I had called them out on their problematic remarks. Life felt disastrous and I worried that I might never feel comfortable. Even my relationship with my dad had become a source of distress.

Instead of finding comfort around him like I was used to, I began painfully overanalyzing how our relationship was supposed to work. When I was his daughter, it was normal for me to hang on him, kiss him, and play with his ears. (I have always loved how bendy his ears are.) As a grown man, I wasn't sure if society would take so kindly to that type of affection. I had rarely seen men interact that way. Beyond childhood, most fathers and sons I had seen weren't affectionate at all, yet I couldn't stand the thought of embracing my dad with a disconnected handshake.

When he started calling me "mate" instead of "love," I couldn't figure out if he was trying to validate my gender or if he too felt awkward on account of the new expectations of our relationship. I was completely lost. We had always been like two peas in a pod, and I hated not feeling permission to embrace our relationship like we once had. The isolation I was already experiencing was compounded by the fracture in our bond. *How was I ever going to be a man if I couldn't even figure out how to act around my own dad?*

I found slight reprieve when I spoke with my mom, but our efforts were slow-moving. We'd FaceTime on the weekends or I'd call her on my way home from work, spending hours poring over my struggles with the social implications of my new identity. I missed the closeness with my dad, but this newfound bond with my mom was a welcomed shift. We had struggled in my younger years, yet now it felt different. The distance I felt as her daughter no longer existed, and I was relieved to have found connection with someone close to me. "Just keep being the wonderful person you are. It doesn't matter what anyone else thinks," she would tell me encouragingly. *I'm trying, Mom, I'm trying.*

Beach day with mom

ARE THERE ANY NON-PHYSICAL DIFFERENCES BETWEEN ME AND CISGENDER MEN THAT YOU'VE NOTICED?

"Yeeeeeessss yes yes yes. Emotionality, a lot of tenderness, more sensitivity (not just with your own emotions but in how you treat others), more openness, less masquerading, higher amounts of communication, more silliness. And that time you pirouetted through the crowd rushing to the dance floor when Mariah Carey came on."

Julia / Partner, Friend / Austin

"You're certainly more compassionate and understanding than most white men. Working with you was such a nice experience because I felt like you were actually listening . . . most guys I work with just want to talk over me."

Andrea / Coworker, Friend / New Jersey

"You tend not to conform to this trend that some cisgender men partake in where they try to project their alpha traits or personality onto others. You're able to create a nice, healthy balance during social settings and that is something that needs acknowledgment."

John / Coworker, Friend / New Jersey

"Yes. I remember feeling significantly safer and more comfortable (and I don't mean physically) to exist in my being than I normally feel around cisgender men. I always notice what feels like a warm breeze of . . . not feeling the gap, the effort, of having to explain who I am, how I live, things I've experienced, etc., to you. Which I of course then have felt . . . selfish for in a way? Because I know there are ways you've had to effortfully verbalize who you are to me in ways that I do not have to."

Amber / Friend / Massachusetts

"The only thing coming to mind that differentiates you is your willingness and desire to sit and just socialize, with talking and connecting being the main event. Most cisgender men I have met (with a handful of beautiful exceptions) tend to relate to socializing differently, and you can see in their eyes that it requires a conscious effort versus a natural state of being, which you sink into when you communicate. IMO, that is your personality and not your gender, especially having met your father . . . . But that is what I have to share!"

Jacqueline / Sister-in-Law, Friend / New Jersey

CHAPTER 12

One of Us

On a lonely Friday night with Bailee a few weeks after another isolating trip home, a title on Netflix caught my eye as I was scrolling. The documentary, titled *One of Us*, was summarized with the text: "In the wake of trauma and abuse, three Hasidic Jews face ostracism, anxiety and danger as they attempt to leave their ultra-Orthodox community." I eagerly hit SELECT on the remote and pulled a blanket over me and Bailee as the film started. I was soon enthralled by the harsh journeys that these three people had embarked on. There was so much pain and so much isolation. Vastly different from my experience, yet not unfamiliar.

Toward the end, there was a scene of one of the male individuals at a Jewish community event. His hair was now short on the sides and he was wearing street clothes. He was standing alone behind a group that was dressed in head-to-toe traditional Hasidic garb. They were all dancing joyously in a circle holding hands. His face was blank and he looked out of place. As the camera continued to show angles of the joyous event, the man explained, "I thought it would be easy and it's not easy. I don't think I'm actually ready to live in a fully secular society. I have this kind of secular anxiety. I'm not blaming the community, I'm not blaming anyone, but I have not found yet what I really want to be a part of." He was no longer recognizable by the Hasidic community based on his new appearance, but he didn't know how to blend into secular society either. He was unsure of where he fit.

I felt a strange sense of relatability to the pain I saw in his eyes. His Jewish community event was my queer bar and his secular society was my straight world. Similar to this man, I had suffered through the isolation that was caused by a brutal shift in my social experience. He and I both faced the same anxieties, regardless of how drastically different our beginnings had been. I had never once considered that other people may also feel isolated by their circumstances. There were individuals out there, albeit not transgender, that felt like they didn't fit in or couldn't quite find their place, just like me. A sense of relief washed over my body. I wasn't completely alone; I just hadn't yet found my place. Falling asleep that night, I felt a little less desperate.

The weeks following, I stepped out into the world with a somewhat different approach. The slight reprieve in my isolation allowed for some space to focus on improving my circumstances. I spoke up more at work and slowly began socializing with my coworkers. I got promoted to associate manager and even began using a gym near my house. There were no male managers there and if I went early enough, the place was nearly empty. My acne had worsened on account of the ever-present stressors, but I was still doing a little better than where it all started.

If I ever did feel unsure of myself, I learned a tool, coined my "bathroom strategy," that proved extremely helpful. I would resort to the nearest bathroom, confirm I was alone, look at myself in the mirror and say out loud, "Get your shit together, James." I would hold eye contact with myself until my confidence returned. Worked like a charm almost every time. I was proud of myself and hopeful that things would keep improving. *Slow but steady wins the race.*

Once my life was seemingly more under control, I set out to find a partner that I could see more regularly. I was desperate for more consistent intimacy and companionship. My relationship with Shanay was slowly losing its magic, the added distance forcing us to face some of the realities of our connection outside of intimacy. I wanted the marriage and the kids, and Shanay didn't. Her job wasn't relocatable, and I had just started mine. We briefly considered moving to Florida together, a place with two primate sanctuaries and ample medical device companies, but it all began to feel like a pipe dream over time. I knew it was time to find someone more compatible with my long-term vision.

Jersey presented a unique challenge for dating. I didn't have an established queer community to socialize with, and the outside world presented many unique challenges I wasn't sure how to navigate. I could not figure out how to connect with women as a man, and their once overt attraction to me was nowhere to be found. With the physical changes of my transition, I had essentially transformed from a sexy "lesbian" to a 5'5", run-of-the-mill dude that women seemingly couldn't care less about. To make matters worse, I suddenly felt like a threat to women in a way I never had before. In my male body, it was no longer acceptable for me to smile or say hello to women and their children. I had to be sure not to stand too close to women in public and leave enough distance when I walked behind them at night. I could no longer openly relate to them about their pains of menstruation or the discomfort of a visit to the OB-GYN. I had no idea how to navigate these strange new interactions.

When I attempted to venture into queer spaces for solidarity, I was met with more complex social nuance. The majority of women assumed I was a gay man, and although this had happened in Austin, facing it alone in Jersey felt exponentially more challenging. My transgender identity was completely skipped over on account of my passing body, and flirtatious glances with women were replaced with men telling me I was a cutie. Instead of women trying to dance with me, men came up behind me and started grinding. They would grab my ass or kiss my cheek while I desperately tried to hold eye contact with women who looked right through me. My ego welcomed the attention from other men, but I resented my inability to exist in the spaces as my true identity, a transgender man who liked women. My prior dysphoria was replaced with foreign insecurities, and I had lost the constant reminder that I was valued. There were no flirty, intoxicating interactions, and I was unable to discern whether I was unattractive to women or this was just how they treated men, gay or straight. The validation that I had once relied on was nowhere to be found.

To make matters worse, I suddenly had an entire world of straight, cisgender men to compare myself to day to day, the work engineers at the forefront. In the past, men had been threatened by me, afraid that I would "steal their girlfriend," and seemingly overnight, I felt completely inadequate standing next to them. My height suddenly mattered, and I worried that my body would never be "masculine" enough to garner the attention of a woman seeking me out as a cis male. I had never felt so undesirable in my life, so I resorted back to online dating for reprieve. At least I could justify why I was slightly more feminine than other men. It was hard to miss the blatant tagline in my profile: "Transman."

"My birth name was Lauren :P," were the first words I ever typed to my now wife. I was drunk scrolling through the app after another unsuccessful night out and her profile had more than caught my eye. She looked gorgeous, down to earth, and most of all, gave off the vibe that she didn't give a fuck what other people thought. *Perhaps I could take a page from her book?* After both mutually "liking" one another, we immediately began messaging back and forth. She was quippy and playful, and her intelligence blatantly shone through her texts. She had a masters from Columbia, and I was impressed. I couldn't wait to meet her and learn more about her fascinating career in social work. I had always admired people who dedicated their lives to the greater good.

In the week between first messaging and meeting in person, I connected with another woman, Ariana. She was fiery, another weakness of mine, and we appeared to have chemistry via text. We met for dinner a few days later, and I was eager to see where it would go. She was chatty and sexy in a mysterious way that intrigued me and left me wanting more. We ended our first date without a kiss on account of my nerves, but did manage to schedule another meet for the upcoming weekend. I was terribly nervous at the thought of Ariana and me being intimate after our next date. *What if she doesn't like my body?* The all too familiar self-doubt began to creep back in. I pushed forward regardless.

Days later, I was sitting across from Ariana at a bar, admiring her form-fitting outfit choice for the evening. We both ordered drinks and ventured into the conversation topic of our dating lives as we sat down. I briefly spoke of prior partners and how difficult it had been to figure out how to date as a transman in Jersey. Ariana went on to talk of her dating history, casually mentioning a "Lauren in Jersey City" that she'd recently met online. My jaw nearly hit the table. Considering the queer dating app we'd met on, Her, is nowhere near the size of some mainstream apps like Tinder or Bumble, I knew immediately we were speaking to the same Lauren. "Wait, I've been speaking to a Lauren in Jersey City. What if we are speaking to the same girl?" I exclaimed. Ariana laughed in response.

Apparently, she and Lauren had already figured it out over text that week. "There aren't many Australian transmen in Jersey City named James," she joked. The date quickly shifted, and I felt a slight pull of jealousy as a result. Ariana would surely choose Lauren over me, and that meant Lauren would drop off too. It didn't help that they spent the entire night texting one another after we acknowledged the mutual connection. Going to bed that night felt more lonely than usual.

The following Tuesday, Ariana and I were sitting on a wall waiting for Lauren to show up for Taco Tuesday. The impending discomfort seemed worth the sacrifice for the possibility of a social life. Friends were better than no friends. While we waited, Ariana voiced her concern that Lauren would be more interested in me than her. My heart dropped slightly. She clearly had written off any interest in her and I being an item. "Don't worry," I assured her. "I don't stand a chance against you. Women aren't really interested in me like they used to be." We sat in silence until Lauren came strolling up with a confidence that reminded me of someone I knew in my past. *Me.* She was dressed slightly more masculine than I expected, yet had a face so striking it was hard not to stare. Minutes into dinner, it was immediately apparent that Lauren wasn't there for me either. The dinner turned out to be a date between Ariana and Lauren, with me as the uncomfortable third wheel. I couldn't blame either of them. Ariana was hot, and Lauren was gorgeous and engaging in a rare way. I didn't stand a chance.

That weekend, Ariana was out of town, so I asked Lauren if she wanted to go to the beach just the two of us. I was eager to explore the Jersey Shore, and I still wanted to connect with her, regardless of our potential for dating. That seemed to be off the table. The next morning, I pulled up at her house, nervous yet excited for us to get to know one another. Lauren plopped in, confidently throwing her stuff into my back seat. I was immediately taken by her electric energy next to me. I hadn't felt it the other night; we were both too distracted. From the moment she got in, we never stopped talking.

Lauren told me about her family, her career, and the highs and lows of her early twenties. I told her of my Australian roots, my cross country moves, and the story of my transition up to that point.

"It's nice to actually get to know each other this time," I teased her. "You didn't ask me a single question the night we met."

She laughed in response. "I thought you were competition!" she insisted, referring to our nonexistent vie for Ariana's attention.

"Oh please, there was no competition and you know it. Maybe a few years ago I would have stood a chance," I joked back.

We soon arrived at Asbury Park, one of Jersey's queer beach towns, and set down our things far away from other people. We needed privacy to explore our newly found connection.

After we got settled, Lauren took off her shirt and shorts, revealing the most incredible hourglass body I have ever seen. Her skin was soft, and she had beautifully detailed tattoos that melded together in a way that mine didn't. I suddenly felt completely intimidated by her presence, although our conversation continued to flow. I felt like Lauren and I had known each other for years. We felt similarly on mostly every topic, and it was almost unbelievable how compatible we were. *Was it possible that I could date a woman like this?* It felt unlikely, but I was eager to find out.

As the hours passed and we grew hotter, we mutually decided to take a dip in the ocean. It was August and the East Coast waters were warm. I ran down to the water, Lauren following not far behind me. The waves offered a nice relief from the sun and a break from my building nerves. The distraction didn't last long. Lauren soon came up behind me, splashing water at me and laughing. I was in awe of her smile, and the way her eyes lit up when she looked at me. My heart pounded as she drew closer. As I braced for an upcoming wave, Lauren jumped on my back, wrapping her arms tight around my shoulders. *I can't believe this gorgeous creature is touching me,* I thought as my body froze. I literally couldn't move any part of me to embrace her. She quickly jumped off, assuming I wasn't interested. We would laugh about it years later, me rejecting Lauren's first advance. "I wanted it so badly, but was too nervous!" I would eventually admit to her.

We wrapped up our glorious beach day as the sun dipped lower and headed back to Jersey City for dinner. As was the case on the way down, we talked the entire drive back. I didn't even mind that the music was off. Lauren's intellect was captivating. I had never met someone that I loved listening to so much. Once we got to dinner, we spent hours speaking about our identities and aspirations for the future over a shared Greek salad and margaritas. It soon grew dark, so I offered to drive

Lauren home after we finished eating. When we arrived at her apartment, we stood outside my car staring at each other for minutes before I made a move. I leaned in to kiss her, doing everything to stop my body from freezing again. She leaned in too, and I couldn't wait to feel her lips on mine. Our first kiss turned out to be hilariously bad. We were both painfully nervous and our shared onion breath didn't help things. We rushed through it, feeling self-conscious that there were people nearby. "I'll see you soon." I smiled at her as she swiped into her building. I couldn't wait to be in her presence again.

From that day forward, Lauren and I were mostly inseparable. We didn't claim monogamy right away, although we did eventually move in that direction. Lauren saw Ariana a few more times while I desperately tried and failed to end my relationship with Shanay on an amicable note. I was saddened by the loss, yet excited to build a life with a partner who wanted the same things I did. Lauren and I wasted no time jumping right in. She moved into my apartment within a matter of months, both of us commenting on how easily we lived together. We seemed to have a perfect harmony that came naturally in a way that neither of us had ever experienced. Our connection was unique and vastly complex, and I can't do it justice with words.

The more time Lauren and I spent together, the less lonely the East Coast felt. I finally had something to look forward to after a busy day at work. After an hour and a half in traffic, I would arrive to Lauren waiting for me. Her commute was much shorter than mine, so she always beat me home. She'd run up to the apartment and take care of Bailee, who was still getting over her adorable jealousy. Lauren was desperately trying to get on Bailee's good side by taking her on walks, us often chatting on the phone the whole time. We still hadn't run out of things to talk about. On Thursday nights, instead of meeting Lauren at home, I'd meet her at our local hang, Liberty Bar. We'd spend hours there enjoying happy hour apps and margaritas, chatting with the bartenders we'd befriended. We made a small circle of friends, mostly other regulars, but kept to ourselves outside of that. Life was easier that way.

Our first Pride together

Lauren's short haircut and overall aesthetic combined with my somewhat effeminate nature led many people to believe we were either gay best friends or siblings. I was forced to either come out or leave people to their assumptions. It all became quite frustrating over time. We both grew exhausted by the notion that we had to somehow justify our relationship to the outside world, both straight and queer. *Why can't we just be two people who are falling madly in love?* There didn't need to be an explanation, and we gravitated toward those who didn't need one. Our existing friends and family clearly saw how perfect we were for one another. Everyone was ecstatic for what we had found, my parents especially grateful that they could accidentally screw up on my name without repercussion. "We were talking to Lauren," they'd joke when we FaceTimed them in California.

My name provided quite the icebreaker for Lauren's family during our first meet, too. One of her sisters had married a James, and two of her nephews were named James and Bennett. In another strange coincidence, Fiona, her niece, was born on the same day I started testosterone in 2015. It was eerie how much crossover there was, serving as a comical point of connection during our first meet.

After many months together, Lauren finally agreed to bring me along to her Italian family's weekly tradition, Sunday Sauce. She had gone solo for months, nervous that she'd introduce me too soon. She had her fair share of failed relationships too. "Don't worry," I told her, "I'm not going anywhere." Perhaps she hadn't realized I was too in love with her to even consider it.

The first Sunday meet was intimidating to say the least. Her family was so much bigger than mine and included her mom and dad, three sisters, two husbands, one now ex-boyfriend that is no longer in the picture, and five little ones. Besides Lauren and Jacqueline, her youngest sister, the rest of the family lived within a one-mile radius of one another. The older two sisters even shared a property line and took down the fence so the kiddos could play. I had never seen anything like it, and I was desperately hopeful I'd fit in. They had all been supportive and happy to hear about Lauren's new beau, although there were questions. Lauren had dated men and women prior, but never a transgender person. Where did I fit? Lauren did her best to answer, and we both chalked up the inquiries to harmless curiosity. It's not every day that somebody brings home a partner like me.

As we pulled up at her parent's house, I saw a sea of people bustling about through the curtains. "I'm so nervous," I told Lauren as we got out of the car. "Don't worry, babe, you'll be fine. They'll love you as much as I do." I looked at her, concerned. "I guess we'll find out!" We were soon inside, taking off our shoes, me shaking more hands than I had in quite some time. They all welcomed me warmly, her mom and sisters even coming in for hugs. Lauren was right, once again. They were friendly, and I appreciated that neither of the husbands were the overt masculine type I disliked. We sat for hours, talking about my family and theirs, my transgender identity never a focal point. Intermittently, if Lauren saw me struggling to remain confident, she would lock eyes with me across the table and nod with her warm "just be yourself" smile. A sweet reminder that I was worthy.

After dinner wrapped up, I hugged everyone goodbye, the men included. I looked forward to the next Sunday Sauce. The pasta and mutz were to die for, and her family wasn't so bad either. *Just kidding, I love them.* Lauren and I made the trek up to Ridgewood often, as long as we were in town. We traveled frequently, and the closer we grew, the more equipped I became to deal with my insecurities. Lauren never allowed me to sit alone with my perceived inadequacy for long, whether we were discussing work or on a beach somewhere. "Don't be silly," she would say when I expressed my concern with the size of my feet. "What if people notice how small they are when they walk by our lounge chairs?" She would hug me and remind me, "Nobody is even paying attention to that, I promise you."

Considering how often she is asked, here are Lauren's thoughts on dating a transman:

James makes me laugh, drives me crazy, and surprises me with coffee and a bagel when I lazily sleep in. James cracks eggs too hard, is sappy, hates clothing that is too thick or not breathable, and roams around when brushing his teeth. James drives too fast, listens to horrible music at ear-bleeding volumes, and smiles to himself when he's being clever. James loves more deeply and authentically than anyone I have ever witnessed. I never need to worry about the toilet seat being left up, and James literally feels my pain when I am a bloated, emotional lump each month. James empathizes in a way that is not male or female but profoundly and uniquely James. He questions everything and hates when things don't make sense.

James dances like no other white man I know; he moves with a suave and flowing energy that is normally reserved for women and Latin men.

All in all, dating a transman is pretty similar, yet profoundly different than dating any other human. That is the whole point, right? We aren't just asked what we want and then matched up accordingly. If that were the case, I would likely never have gotten my loud Australian with an affinity for corgis, cycling, and Trader Joe's meatless breakfast patties. I would likely never have gotten my perfect match.

CHAPTER 13

The Vomit Carpet

Lauren's constant support continued to help bolster my self-confidence, but unfortunately, we were far from in the clear. At the end of 2018, about six months into our relationship, my company announced the acquisition of another company down in Virginia. Suddenly, I was forced to start my experience in New Jersey all over again, and I was not ready for it. The integration meant a whole new group of people to learn how to interact with, and I began crumbling at the thought. I had spent the last year acclimating to my coworkers in Jersey, and the pressure of learning the new site in Virginia was the last thing I needed. The added anxiety of this new chapter in my professional life triggered the start of a rough decline in my physical well-being. Lauren was desperately unsure of how to help. I simply hadn't made enough progress to counter another drastic shift in circumstances.

After arriving in Virginia a few months into the acquisition, I went straight to a meeting with three other men, two senior whatevers and my boss. My stomach had been hurting for many weeks, and I was overall quite unwell. The four of us sat in a small office mostly exchanging small talk before we moved on to anything work related. "How's the wife? How are the kids? Did you see the [insert dumb sport here] game?" I had grown sick of this same set of predictable questions. As usual, they were void of any actual connection, and I felt mostly unable to contribute. I wasn't married, didn't have kids, and couldn't care less about sports. Instead, I sat there painfully overanalyzing every aspect of my being, much as I had the night before I started in Jersey.

When we moved on from the dreaded small talk and shifted to integration planning, I had no choice but to participate. As I spoke, I was consumed with worry over the way my voice sounded and how I moved my hands. I was convinced that they would think I was too animated or effeminate. Their voices were octaves deeper than mine and none of them moved their hands like I did. I worried that they would question my intelligence as I wasn't an engineer like them. Sweat formed in my temples; I didn't want them studying me too closely. *Something is off about James,* they would think. I lost focus at multiple points during the meeting. My stomach panged with pain and my chest tightened. I grew increasingly hotter as the minutes passed.

Following the meeting, I left the office and immediately went back to the hotel. I didn't care that the decision was a poor professional choice. I had to get myself together or there wouldn't be anything left of me for a job. I called my dad and he listened intently while I babbled through my tears. Eventually, the nausea got the best of me and forced me to end the call. Once we were off the phone, I attempted to eat dinner and then proceeded to throw up all over the floor of my hotel room. The vomit matched the color of the carpet. *Gross.* I called Lauren, panicked, and we agreed that I should go to the nearest urgent care. She asked if she should drive down from Jersey, her voice full of concern. I declined her offer. I would call her after I had spoken to a doctor. I headed downstairs to the lobby, frantic and embarrassed. The kind front desk staff coordinated a taxi for me. I was too worked up to operate the dumb Lyft app.

When I arrived at the urgent care, I had trouble explaining my symptoms. All I knew was that I had thrown up and I wasn't okay. They did blood tests and asked me a slew of questions. The more time passed, the more I regretted ever leaving my hotel room. I hadn't even had time to put cover up on my shitty skin, and the lighting in the room exacerbated its redness. My tears enhanced the already problematic inflammation, and I was disgusted when I saw my reflection in the mirror. I wanted to be alone, but I couldn't just get up and leave.

After an hour or two of waiting, the diagnosis came back. Anxiety. *Great job, James. You've made yourself sick with all of this worrying.* The doctor gave me a few Xanax tablets and I was on my way. I called Lauren, both relieved and ashamed at the doctor's answer. I quickly packed up my things and flew back to Jersey the next morning, drowning in hopeless defeat the entire flight home. Something had to change. This trajectory was no longer sustainable, and I had come way too far to give up.

After arriving home, I attempted, and failed, for the next few months to find a Russell 2.0 in Jersey. In unison, I made an appointment with a gastroenterologist to rule out any actual issue with my stomach. A professional opinion seemed like a good place to start. The doctor suggested I get an endoscopy to be sure nothing serious was going on, regardless of my admitted stress levels. *A $2000 peace of mind check. Fun.* When the results of the endoscopy came back as "Inconclusive, General Inflammation," I felt a strange combination of relief and despair. *I have to be able to do something to make this better.* I turned my attention to the next controllable factor in my life, my diet.

Considering this is not a book about transgender dietary choices, I will spare you the intricate details. Long story short, I tried a few different elimination diets and ultimately found that after a month with no meat, my stomach issues mostly resolved. From there, my anxiety also got a much-needed break. Whether my anxiety declined from the significant absence of stomach issues or the lack of cortisol levels from the meat I'm not sure, but I finally had a smidge of emotional capacity back on my side. The tides began to turn, and I pretty much never ate meat again. Yet for whatever reason, I still have an extremely hard time saying no to pork when I'm drunk.

By the middle of 2019, I had gotten to a reasonably good place and Lauren and I decided to make the move from our tenth floor apartment in Jersey City to a suburban neighborhood on the outskirts. We both wanted to get away from the bustle of the downtown area, and a little extra space couldn't hurt. Bailee had been begging for a yard ever since I left Texas. We were all so excited that Lauren and I hadn't taken the time to consider how this new environment would feel. Our new home literally had a white picket fence and a whole lot of unexpected heteronormative conventions to adjust to. We were suddenly surrounded by straight, cisgender couples, most of them decades older than us.

Regardless of our confusing identities, neither of us had ever lived anywhere so "straight" before. Lauren handled it well, but I felt like I'd entered another gauntlet of social norms. My insecurities quickly started to get the best of me again, regardless of my mostly pescatarian diet. I worried incessantly that people in the community would wonder why Lauren was with me. She was gorgeous, successful, and confident, and I was weak, short, and feminine. All the progress I had made suddenly seemed frozen in time. *Not again.*

One night while on an evening walk with Bailee around the block, Lauren and I ran into our neighbors, Trish and Angelo. I mustered up a quiet "hello" and brushed past them quickly. I had been avoiding them for weeks and didn't plan on stopping then.

"Why don't you talk much when we interact with them?" Lauren asked me as we continued walking. "You are usually so confident and chatty, but when we are around them, you barely say anything," she pressed on. "Trish clearly loves Bailee. Why do you always avoid her in the yard or when we see her around?"

I could feel my blood begin to boil. How dare she question my efforts. "You are being so insensitive," I responded. "Don't you see how much I have already overcome?"

She looked perplexed. "I'm not saying that. I'm saying that you should just be yourself. You are a wonderful person and they won't be able to see that if you don't show them."

I was so angry with myself and knew I had to do better. If not for me, then for Lauren.

My "only way out is through" mentality kicked back in again, hard. The next time we saw Trish and Angelo on our evening walk, I deliberately stopped to converse with them. For the first time in any interaction with them, I truly participated. I hated the way my voice sounded and obsessed over what the husband thought of me. "James is so feminine, isn't he?" Angelo would no doubt say to Trish as we walked away. "Yes, they are an odd couple," Trish would surely respond. I pushed away the negative thoughts. This had to happen. Angelo owned an Italian restaurant nearby, so I started there.

"Are you both free for dinner this weekend?" I asked, shakily.

"Yep!" Trish responded excitedly.

"Should I set up a reservation at Angelo's restaurant?" I nodded.

"That would be great. We are looking forward to it."

We wished them goodnight and continued along the path. Once out of earshot, I turned to Lauren and asked, "Aren't you proud of me?" beaming at my own success.

"Yes! That was great!" she exclaimed, showering me with validation.

Dinner was wonderful and the positive interactions continued from there. Trish and Angelo lived in the townhouse above ours, so we essentially shared a backyard. There was a fence in between, but we freely moved back and forth. They were quite the socialites in the community, often inviting other couples over for drinks. My chest tightened when we met new people, some clearly confused by Lauren and me, but it got easier over time. Once they realized we were together, everyone moved on. I learned to just be myself; that really was the only option anyway. I chatted with the women and eventually grew more comfortable with the men. As always, I struggled to understand the men's version of connection, but learned to participate in a way that felt right to me. I avoided any talk I didn't want to be a part of and eventually appreciated the ways in which they bonded. We would tease each other, Angelo often squeezing my shoulders as a sign of affection.

On account of the constant exposure, I began to feel more comfortable at work, too. It wasn't healthy to focus on the things that made me "different," both socially and physically, and it was unlikely that my coworkers gave a shit about those things anyways. I realized that no one at work probably ever noticed how small my feet were or that the bulge in my pants was nonexistent. There was most likely nothing "off" about me; I only focused on those things because they were relevant to me as a transgender man. Once I stopped obsessing over my physical "inadequacies," I began to notice that my body wasn't really all that unique after all. There were many men at work that were the same height and shape as me, if not only an inch or two taller. Some of them weren't even as fit as I was. Not everyone was a 6'5" giant with a superhero physique, size 12 feet, and hands the size of my head.

I did all I could to stop focusing on my voice, mannerisms, or the nagging concern that everyone thought I was gay. I learned to hold my body confidently and sit how I wanted. People were going to think what they wanted, and all I could control was being a good guy and doing my job well. I decided to just be myself and surprisingly, found the results quite rewarding. Female coworkers started to call me a gentleman and comment on how thoughtful I was. They appeared to value my lack of concern with the expectations of masculinity. When I was with men, I stopped putting so much pressure on myself to connect with them if it felt unnatural to me. It was okay for me to not like or want to talk about sports. I wanted to engage on an emotionally deeper level, so I pushed for those types of conversations instead.

There were roadblocks, of course, like the time a male coworker told me I shouldn't tell other men I was "excited to see them," but it all got easier over time. Plus I had my handy bathroom strategy just in case. I continued to find validation as I settled more into myself. My confidence soared, and finally, for the first time in my life, I just existed. It was nothing short of glorious, and the rewards kept on coming. I excelled at work and eventually left my company for an opportunity at a small, private one also based in Jersey. Lauren and I struggled to make queer friends, but we had the reliable adoration of the straights in our life to rely on.

At Trish's fiftieth birthday party a year or so after we moved in, one of our male neighbors told Lauren and I that we were beautiful together. "You don't see couples like you nowadays," he said with a genuine smile as he watched us. Later that same evening, Trish's seventy-three-year-old mother, Marietta, told me while we danced together, "I love the way you move your lower half." Lauren and I still laugh about it years later.

SPILLING THE T

HOW DID YOU PERCEIVE MY IDENTITY WHEN WE FIRST MET?

"I initially thought you were a cisgender gay man. I was excited! I thought, awesome, another gay in the office, and he's cute! When you told me you were trans and had a girlfriend, I was a little bit bummed (only because of the crush I had on you), but I was still so excited to get to know you and have a new friend at work and living nearby."

Kevin / Coworker, Friend / New Jersey

"I thought you were gay (lol) and then I heard you say 'my girlfriend' at a meeting. I was so confused, looked around, but I was the only one confused!! I figured they knew something I didn't."

Lilly / Coworker, Friend / New Jersey

"I assumed you were a cisgender man. I had a feeling you were queer, but wasn't sure where you fell under the LGBT+ umbrella."

Deirdre / Coworker, Friend / New Jersey

"I'll start this by saying, I am super oblivious in general. And not like in the good 'I don't see gender' type of way. I am just generally an airhead and was just happy to have a friend to drink and have fun with. I do remember thinking you were a bit effeminate, both in mannerisms and drink choice (lemon drop), but we bonded over beers and smokes, we were talking about girls, BMWs, and a shared love of pilsners so I didn't give it much thought past that. Also, the pool was fun as hell even though I sucked."

John / Non-Pool Shark, Coworker, Friend / New Jersey

"Good question. I couldn't figure you out. I didn't know if you and Lauren were a couple or roommates. First I thought you were gay, but once I saw the relationship, I just chocked it up to you being Australian. Sometimes people from other countries are different than Americans. LMAO."

Trish / Neighbor, Friend / New Jersey

CHAPTER 14

The Pita Chip Man

Ten years before transitioning, back in high school, I once had a friend say, "Lauren, you have made me realize that gay people aren't much different than I am." She continued on with a smile, "You helped normalize what it means to be gay." Prior to meeting me, Sam had never been close with any gay people. It wasn't from a position of homophobia; she just hadn't had the exposure. Gay people had always been the "other," whether Sam meant for it to be that way or not. After becoming friends with me that summer, she was able to break through a barrier she didn't even know she had.

Throughout our time together, Sam realized that although my sexual identity was not the same as hers, we weren't really all that different. We both liked the beach, frozen yogurt, Mexican food, Starbucks, and drinking shitty alcohol out of plastic bottles with our friends. We both shared a similar sense of humor and the same deep love for our families. The fact that I liked women and she liked men was entirely irrelevant. I never set out to help her achieve this realization, it just happened naturally. Years later, as a passing transgender man, my life became a slightly altered version of that summer, albeit not always as carefree.

Once I had found comfort in myself by the end of 2019, coming out was nowhere near as anxiety-provoking as it once was. Instead of fear, I felt proud of who I was and wanted to share myself with the world. Queer people still didn't recognize me or validate my relationship with Lauren, but I found immense value on the other side of my passing privilege. If I didn't come out right away and people got to know me as James, they were naturally challenged to reassess their beliefs, paradigms, and preconceived notions of what it means to be transgender when I did.

A majority of the straight people I interacted with every day had never really been exposed to the queer community beyond a few gay and lesbian friends. They were uninformed and had limited experience interacting with transgender individuals. They didn't have concrete political views regarding the bathroom bill debate, but they also probably hadn't thought much about it. It wasn't relevant to them. They believed in equal rights for all people, but hadn't delved into exactly what that means. If I didn't come out right away, a different light suddenly shone on "James" once they knew my beginnings. To future potential allies like these, I was just a presumably cisgender guy that they had no reason to believe was any different from them.

Inevitably, a conversation topic would come up and I'd have my opportunity to weave my transgender identity into the discussion. *Surprise!* The responses have been varied, yet mostly positive. People often express surprise and say things like, "I had no idea" or "That's amazing." My favorite was a boss, yogurt spoon hovering midair, who exclaimed, "I'm so sorry, James, that is just the last thing I was expecting you to say." Others respond with flippant statements like, "This changes nothing" or (one of the gems) "It doesn't matter to me. It's as if you told me your favorite color was blue." They then apologize for acting with disregard or inadvertently minimizing my experience. I assure them that I understand; the value of the moment has already been achieved. Every transgender person may not look like me or me them, but I have potentially "normalized" the identity for someone.

My family, particularly my parents, adopted a similarly powerful response throughout the years following my transition. Beyond the unmatched support of my journey, they navigated all questions, probing or curious, without an ounce of shame. "I thought you had a son and daughter?" acquaintances would inquire when they spoke of James and Jonathan. "Yes, and now we have two sons," they would reply without missing a beat. *There really isn't anywhere a person can go with that.* I felt guilty on account of their potential discomfort, but neither of them seemed all that concerned. They had nothing to be ashamed of, they assured me. In response to a lady who asked my dad at a dinner party, "How does James have sex?" he simply said, "Well." *Thanks, Dad. You're a legend.*

My everything

Even my grandparents stayed hot with the support. When the four of us, Lauren included, visited England for my grandma's ninetieth birthday, my grandma proudly told everyone, "James is now a transvestite," in preparation for my arrival. The language may have been wrong, but the meaning was right. Their friends and our extended family were a tad shocked, even awkwardly mistaking Lauren as me during the party, but my family stood their ground. They all embraced me proudly during the many photos taken during the event. This lack of shame, demonstrated by the very people that society expects to be most shameful, was powerful beyond measure. My family still loved me and so should the rest of the world. This type of unconditional love works wonders to change people's perceptions, and every transgender person deserves the type of support I have.

I gave prompts to my parents and my brother, and as expected, my dad and brother ignored it while my mom followed it to a tee.

Dad

I have very fond memories of seeing Lauren grow up. Throughout the years, we have done a lot of things together, and I can honestly say all I have is fun and happy memories. I did not see or think of Lauren as anything other than a fun-loving daughter.

During the time leading up to her teens, I never saw or thought anything about Lauren's gender. Yes, there were times when she would say, "I am not wearing that dress," or didn't seem comfortable in a certain dress and seemed to be a bit of a tomboy, but I thought that was just part of the growing up phase. When she reached her early teens, she started to question her sexuality. Little things like, she never seemed too keen to date boys or showed much interest and seemed "somewhat confused." Thankfully, I have always had a fantastic relationship with Lauren and still do to this day, so when she spoke to me about boys and mentioned in a sentence, which I won't forget, "When I see a pretty girl I get butterflies in my stomach," I soon realized where all the confusion was stemming from.

Another time was when I was in the bathroom chatting to Lauren and she broke down and said, "Why did I have to be gay?" I found that moment one of the most traumatic times I have had as a father, seeing my lovely Lauren distraught and not being able to help. It was at that time I remember feeling a little helpless. I couldn't "fix it" for her as dads are supposed to do. What I did know is, I along with Carol, had to be there for her and help her through this. She was still the same person before she thought she was gay, a beautiful fun-loving daughter.

Now moving forward to when Lauren started college. She seemed happy on the surface, she was a pretty girl and did really well at college. Toward the end of college, we noticed a change in Lauren; shorter haircut, dressing a little different, taking on a more manly look, and our conversations were more along the lines of "somewhat confused again." It was at that time she started discussing her sexuality with a psychologist and us. From there, things moved quite rapidly from "being gay" to not identifying with a gender/thinking she was in the wrong body, and that was the time Carol and I thought things could dramatically change direction. We gave Lauren her space to allow her to find out what was going to happen, not because we didn't care, but it is not something you can influence. You just have to be there for support and understanding.

When the discussion came about that Lauren was going to be James, I don't know what I thought, perhaps I was a little in denial. I remember thinking life is difficult enough as it is, but throw into the mix a change of gender and life is never going to be the same for Lauren/James. I remember feeling sad and helpless, but surprisingly embraced the "situation" because it had been a gradual process over the years so it was easier to soak in. Over the proceeding months, Carol and I spoke at length about Lauren and just kept coming back to the same conclusion. We are going to be there for her/him.

I think back over this time and where we are now and question if our relationship had changed, I can honestly say not at all. James said to my wife once that Dad seems to have changed toward me, and I don't think that was the case. I think I was in denial and I suppose I was inwardly processing it. To someone outside, they would think I might have changed. In actuality, our relationship just keeps getting better. Yes, Lauren is now James, but he is still the same lovely person inside and it is really important for people to understand that.

Today, I honestly think of James as James as if he had always been James. Occasionally though, when we are in a restaurant and the waiter says "sir," I do a double take. Other than that, it's like we have a son who is a wonderful, courageous human being and we love him very much.

Brother

During the time Lauren was undergoing his transition to James, I was in my early twenties, immature, and regrettably quite self-absorbed. While I internally supported James in his decision, I was not active in his journey. I had been jealous of his relationship with my parents for many years and was resentful toward him for it. I immaturely convinced myself that the reason I didn't have the strong emotional/personal relationship with my parents I so desired was because of him. Obviously, that was not the case whatsoever.

Over the last several years of growing up, not only did I realize the immaturity of my own personal being, I also started to understand the gravity of James' situation. Prior to his transition, he was living his life as if he was trying to fit his left foot into his right shoe. It just wasn't a fit, and it never was going to be. Simply put, Lauren becoming James made more sense than syrup on pancakes.

Although, the process was not a simple one. I have become even more open-minded and accepting of the LGBTQ community because of my brother's experience. His journey has shed light on the hardships and battles the LGBTQ community must deal with head-on, every day. Seeing my brother overcome obstacles and difficulties (most will never surmount) has provided me with much needed perspective. I will never shoot someone down or tell them they're wrong in doing something they believe is true in their heart. For James, it has always been true that he was meant to be a man. Not only am I happy to call him my brother, I am proud to say that his strength and courage have been nothing short of an inspiration to me.

Brothers with Bailee

Mom

1. How would you explain my gender expression as a child?

Children come in all shapes, sizes and personalities, so when your new baby arrives it's best not to have too many preconceived ideas about what the future holds for this latest little newcomer to the world. However, that being said, during my first pregnancy I was so convinced that I was carrying a boy that I had not even considered what I might call the new arrival, should it be a girl. I actually did not have any preference either way and so when Lauren Danielle arrived (names that were chosen about a week after her delivery!), I was delighted to have given birth to a healthy baby girl.

From that day forward until the age of three or four years; Lauren grew and developed into the most beautiful, loving, happy, fun, intelligent and engaging little person—incredibly outgoing and confident. Looking back, my only recollection of anything a little different from the norm in regard to the development of a typical little girl was Lauren's total lack of interest in anything considered "girly," including objections to wearing girly clothes or playing with dolls. She always liked to dress for comfort and preferred jeans or shorts and a T-shirt, to anything that might be considered feminine attire. This trend continued right through Lauren's teenage years, to the point that she was so disinterested in clothes, hair, makeup, etc., that even a suggestion of a trip to the mall to purchase new items was completely dismissed out of hand. In some ways, this did not come as any surprise to me, since I had always been a "tomboy" as a child and also preferred simpler attire, which was more conducive to climbing trees and building camps in the local woods, than excursions to the mall to buy lipsticks, eyeshadow, or the latest in fashion clothing and shoes.

During Lauren's teenage years, up until the age of about sixteen, we experienced very few of the teenage "issues" and parenting challenges that many of our friends seemed to be facing with their teenage daughters. From sixteen onward however, things did start to become more complicated, and Stephen and I were beginning to sense that perhaps Lauren was struggling with feelings that both confused and frustrated her. This became more and more evident when she was faced with invitations from male classmates to school dances and formal events, which required the purchase of very feminine outfits, trips to the hairdresser for an "updo," along with makeup, jewelry, etc. Lauren was never short of male friends or admirers, but it was clear to us that she was struggling with how she was supposed to transform herself into the typical expected stereotype of the high school prom attendee. She did a great job and carried it off perfectly, but as parents, we were very aware of the internal turmoil it was causing her.

Some negative changes to Lauren's behavior at home, the way she reacted to her dad and me, along with her newly formed close relationships with some of her more adventurous and unconventional female school friends, prompted us to sit her down and try to offer some help and reassurances while she was obviously struggling with her own feelings and identity. We had always talked openly about anything and everything, so we had no problem discussing whatever Lauren felt she wanted to talk about, safe in the knowledge that we would not judge or criticize anything she might say.

2. How did you feel when I told you I was transitioning?

When Lauren told us that she was planning to move ahead

with transitioning, I was not at all surprised. I had thought for a while that this was going to be the next step toward Lauren feeling that she could become the person who was already inside of her waiting to be reborn. Stephen and I had discussed this possibility already and had so many questions and concerns, not only about the physical impact to Lauren's body but the ongoing difficulties and challenges that she would likely be facing for the rest of her life. We began to read and research information on how this process would take place, and were filled with apprehension and concerns about the journey Lauren was about to embark upon; but knowing that there was no other choice for her, we were prepared to offer as much support and encouragement as we possibly could.

3. How did my transition change our relationship?

Every parent wants their child to be happy; but life and relationships are anything but easy and we knew that having a child who was going to transition would awaken emotions and challenges that as parents we had not previously experienced. We just hoped that we would have the emotional capacity to be able to focus on Lauren's needs and be able to give the support that we knew would be needed. Any person who is brave enough to put themselves through this process deserves unquestionable love and support from family and friends, although sadly this is often not the case.

Accepting the realization that our daughter of twenty-five years was stepping away from that part of her life and almost starting over was a situation that we initially struggled to come to terms with, but we reminded ourselves often that this was the same wonderful person on the inside and it was just the outside appearance that would be changing. For the longest time we continued to talk about Lauren instead of James when we were not in his company, and this was something that took a while and a considerable amount of conscious effort to overcome!

4. How did my transition affect your life and relationships?

At the beginning of the transition process, Lauren (still Lauren at that point!) sent an email to all of our family and friends explaining what was going to be happening. The response was overwhelmingly one of support and admiration from most quarters, which was really heartwarming. A few friends were less accepting of the situation and seemed unwilling to consider that there was no other choice for Lauren but to go ahead with the transition process—it was a necessity. A few even suggested that this was just a "phase" that would be overcome. Stephen and I had anticipated and expected this reaction from some people and had already decided that we would not be discussing the opinions of the few, which are based on an understandable amount of ignorance about the situation. Many people have never had any interaction with or ever known a person close to them who has transitioned, and would be reluctant to ask questions or be willing to try and understand.

A couple of my friends still struggle with inquiring after James or even acknowledging the change of name. I try not to let this affect my relationships with these friends, but it's not an easy thing to do. There have often been situations where I see acquaintances I may not have seen or spoken to in a while, and I can't remember whether they are aware of Lauren's transition. If I feel the time is right, I may make reference to this without going into detail, but simply stating a fact in passing conversation. If questions are asked, then I am always happy to talk further, knowing that this will not be a five-minute conversation! At the end of the day, the transition is about the person who is living the changes day to day and not about that person's family or friends, and their thoughts and opinions. To hear your child tell you that when they look at themselves in the mirror, they finally see the person they always imagined they should be, is something that elevates your heart to a place that helps you overcome everything else.

As much as I grew to love being out in comfortable environments, I found the greatest value in exposing my identity was in response to bigotry. Unfortunately, there's a whole subset of society that isn't like Sam, my sweet boss, or my family. The people who aren't just uninformed or unaware, but are dead set on hating everything different from them. The transphobic assholes. The mostly white, cisgender straight men behind the bathroom bills and constant barrage of hateful, toxic language. The ones that hide behind religion and unsubstantiated claims of transgender people wanting to do anything other than relieve their bladder in a bathroom. Ironically, most of these people have no idea I'm transgender until I tell them. I look nothing like the transgender women that threaten their fragile masculinity so intensely. Instead, I appear as "one of them."

An interaction I once had on a plane perfectly sums up this influence I stumbled upon. I was on a flight down to New Orleans, sitting next to a generic straight, white, cis businessman. *My favorite.* Once we had reached cruising altitude, the flight attendants began their distribution of drinks and snacks. As I looked down the aisle, I noticed something unique about ours. She was transgender like me, albeit not yet passing. I watched her nervously as she traversed the busy aisle, dodging feet and elbows. She had a few inches on my 5'5" and her frame was slender, yet strong. I recognized the look in her eyes as they darted around at all the passengers while simultaneously avoiding legitimate eye contact with anyone.

I glanced at the man next to me, eager to see if he had noticed her too. He was consumed by his laptop screen, but I knew it wouldn't be long before he looked up. The flight attendant was almost to our row, my body tensing with each step she took. A sense of dread had overtaken me. I desperately hoped my neighbor would treat her with respect, but I knew that was unlikely. Men like him didn't have the greatest track record based on my experience. Especially when it comes to transgender women. I felt relieved as she handed him his drink and "Bistro Box." It seemed a little too early to be drinking, but I rescinded my judgment when I remembered he at least wasn't the manspreading type. *I will never understand the need for cis, straight men to take up so much space.* As the flight attendant handed me the coffee I had asked for, I desperately tried and failed to hold her eye contact. I missed the opportunity to reassure her that she wasn't alone.

As she continued down the aisle, my neighbor nudged me. *Here come the transphobic comments,* I braced myself as I turned to him. "Do you want these?" he said as he handed me his small bag of pita chips. "Sure, thank you!" I responded with concealed relief while trying not to sound too feminine. *God forbid I gave this man any reason to find me odd.* I pulled myself out of my thoughts and focused back on my newly acquired snack. *What a shame, he must be on one of those no-carb diets,* I entertained myself in an attempt for distraction.

Thankfully, the rest of the flight was uneventful. The pita chip man worked diligently while I fretted about my work trip. I was thankful when we landed, both to provide a distraction from my anxieties and put an end to my concern that my neighbor was going to say something to me about our flight attendant. The plane finally came to a halt, and I looked ahead anxiously as people deplaned at a pace slower than I will ever understand. As my eyes circled the plane's patrons, I inadvertently caught a glimpse of my neighbor's phone screen. "She's probably wearing the scarf to cover up her Adam's apple," screamed out to me from one of the blue outgoing message bubbles. *A sledgehammer of judgment.*

My body grew hot with searing anger while I read through the rest of the texts between him and his friend. My naive optimism had been crushed in a moment. He was just another transphobic asshole after all. *Don't say anything, James. It isn't worth it.* I pictured the man getting angry with me, veins bulging out all over his massive hands and forehead. He would quite predictably start an altercation in front of all the people on the plane, and I had to avoid that at all costs. Violence was not the answer, and I most certainly would not come out on top. He was probably at least a hundred pounds heavier than me.

While I desperately searched my mind for a solution, I recalled that I had seen a name in his email signature earlier in the flight. He seemed *very* busy and *very* important, and I was curious about what company he worked for. I quickly jotted down his details in my phone from memory. I couldn't wait to draft the most beautifully written email I could muster. *This man had to know what he had done.* After navigating all the anxiety-provoking hurdles between the plane and the hotel, I was finally alone to write my masterpiece. This was my only opportunity to expand this man's mind beyond the narrow lane of his own life.

> I know this is strange and borderline inappropriate, but I didn't want to miss a good opportunity to do something I mean to do more often. When we were getting off the flight, I happened to glance over and see your

text message thread. I understand that reading someone's screen isn't okay, but it caught my eye and I did.

I noticed your text had a specific topic, our transgender flight attendant. I understand that this person was clearly not passing and may never, and this is where I come in. I am also transgender. I was born female and began my transition four years ago. Unlike with our flight attendant, you most likely had no idea. I've been fortunate in that way. I was just a guy sitting next to you on the plane that you were kind enough to share your pita chips with.

I need you to know that transgender people are all around you, just trying to live their lives like you are. They just happened to have been born in the wrong body, like myself. Just imagine this was someone you knew, maybe even your kid if you have any. That was the reality for my parents. The flight attendant is just trying to live her truth and doesn't deserve to be a joke between you and whoever you were texting. I appreciate you reading this, and I hope it gets my point across.

J

PS: The other flight attendants were also wearing scarves. It may not have been to cover her Adam's apple. Maybe she's waited her whole life to dress like a woman, just like I did to finally get to wear a suit.

Almost immediately after I hit send, the pita chip man responded. "Thank you for taking the time to call me out and remind me of the diversity of our world. You are absolutely right and I apologize for my insensitive behavior." *One down, millions more to go.* If I can normalize one version of transgender, I imagine that might translate to others less privileged than me. I can't always come out, mostly for fears of physical safety, but when I can, I do. I feel naive writing the words, but I can't help but remain hopeful. If my coming out can change one person's mind about the transgender community, I consider the vulnerability a worthy success.

CHAPTER 15

Eggs before Easter

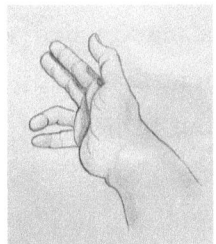

By 2020, my identity felt more settled and Lauren and I were mostly just living life. With the space to focus on other things, we grew more and more eager to make our dreams of living on the sunnier coast a reality. I had always wanted to return home, and Lauren was done with the upset of seasonal depression. I planned to ask my work for a full-time remote position, and Lauren had already initiated the transfer of her clinical license by the time COVID hit. We had coincidentally just returned from a visit to San Diego, our future dream destination, when the world shut down. I was subsequently furloughed for two months and Lauren's last six months at her job were made immeasurably more difficult.

After I returned from my furlough, Lauren and I made the decision to put our plan in motion. We couldn't stand the thought of a quarantined winter and considering my team was functioning well remotely, now felt like the time to ask if I could just stay that way. It didn't matter whether I managed staff from a house in Jersey or a house in California. COVID wasn't going to be over anytime soon, and the prospect of anyone returning to the office felt far off. It was go time, and I could jump on a plane whenever the world returned to normalcy. Management thankfully obliged to my request, and Lauren promptly put in her two-month notice after we received the good news.

We informed our landlord and began the daunting task of organizing a moving POD to ship our belongings, car transfer, and booking of our hotel stays for the week-long cross-country road trip we planned to take. Bailee and Mango, our bearded dragon, were unable to travel by plane and driving across the country seemed to be a safer option overall. In the interim, we had our wedding rings made by a local Jersey City jeweler (*Shoutout to @LoveLocked*) and got engaged. Lauren expressed disdain at the idea of an elaborate proposal and all that mattered to me was us ending up together. I was not in the least worried about the formalities of it all. I ended up unofficially proposing in our doorway with a phone video partially obscured by Bailee's not-so-small midsection. It was undeniably perfect.

A few weeks later, as if to finally grant me a break, United States Citizenship and Immigration Services (USCIS) scheduled my long-awaited naturalization ceremony. It had been rescheduled from months prior on account of another delay to perform the "background check on two identities." Nothing had ever gone smoothly when it came to legal documentation. Since the nightmare "Male Impersonator" appointment in October of 2017, I had been stuck in an absurd holding pattern for almost three years, coming out to confused government employees far too often. As my green card expired in the beginning of 2018, I had to get a fancy little stamp in my passport every six months to prove I was legally in the country. Each time the stamp expired, so would my driver's license. I could write an entire book on all the ridiculous ins and outs of my trips to USCIS and the DMV, but nobody wants to read about that. Here are some of the highlights:

- USCIS Agent #1 asked, "Who's this?" while pointing at my outdated green card photo. "That's me," I responded with as much confidence as I could muster.

- USCIS Agent #2 told me my citizenship was delayed TWO years because "they had to do a background check on two identities."

- USCIS Agent #3 responded, "Well of course you are. You are a totally different person now!" when attempting to empathize with the difficulty I was having with my misaligned documentation. *Thank you, I am aware.*

- DMV Supervisor #1 told me, "You won't have to show

this again," in reference to my outdated IDs. I then had to show the IDs at least three more times.

- DMV Employee #1 reviewed my documents with a bewildered look, handed them back to me, wrote my cell number on a Post-It note (with no name), and dismissively said, "We'll call you." *Needless to say, I never got a call.*

I couldn't wait for it to be over, and in a symbolic twist, the naturalization ceremony was scheduled on my birthday. *The best gift ever.* I officially became federally recognized as James on the same day I came into the world as Lauren thirty-one years prior. I reveled in the relief of reaching the light at the end of a long, humiliating, demoralizing tunnel as I drove home from the ceremony that morning. *Finally, my last trip to USCIS.* It almost didn't feel real.

On September 30, 2020, Lauren, Bailee, Mango, and I set out on our road trip, naturalization certificate safely stowed in the trunk. We shared a tearful goodbye with Trish and Angelo and were on our way. We only made it to Texas before Bailee's car sickness got the best of her, but overall, we did okay. The country was beautiful, sans the Trump propaganda in the first few states. I felt so incredibly proud of myself as I looked around the car. I had left California eight years ago as a woman and was returning as a man with my future wife, a corgi, and a bearded dragon. *You've done well, kid,* I said to myself as my eyes met the rearview mirror.

Goodbye forever, USCIS

After a forty-two-hour drive and Bailee throwing up for most of the distance between Texas and California, we made it to our Airbnb. Lauren started her new job a few days later while I set up my new remote office and looked for our first rental property. We reunited with my friends from high school and college and socialized with my parents often. I grew even closer with my mom and my relationship with my dad slowly fell back into its rightful place. I still played with his ears, and we went racing often. The balance in both relationships has been one of the greatest gifts of my transition.

Nine months after relocating, Lauren and I had scheduled our wedding date, and I set out to get the cream suit of my dreams. I called my dad on the way to my appointment, filled with excitement.

"What are you going to say when they ask you which way you dress?" my dad inquired.

"What? What does that mean?" I responded anxiously. I could hear him smiling through the phone.

"It's what guys ask when they want to know which side of your pants your penis typically falls on." We laughed hysterically together, settling on the left side as my answer.

"Thanks, Dad," I said as I arrived at the store. "I'll call you after." I was nervous, but life's challenges over the prior years had prepared me well.

Upon entering, I met with my "style advisor," Dante. He was friendly, impeccably dressed, and made me feel at ease. *Still unusual for me to find with other men.* "I just can't wear a boring blue, you know what I mean?" I told him. "I totally get it. We are seeing a lot of different suits going out these days. People are branching out from the conventional looks we've seen in the past." *Perfect*, I thought. Dante pulled out a few options before we found what I was looking for. "This is exactly what I want," I told him as I ran my hands over the soft fabric for the first time. I promptly turned around and he draped the jacket over my shoulders. A nice fit, although long on the arms as usual. I smiled as I looked at myself in the mirror. *Is this really what I look like?* Dante handed me the matching pants, and I headed into the dressing room.

As expected, the pants were too long and a tad tight on the tummy. Evidence of my inability to say no to tacos at any point in my life. I took a deep breath and walked out to show Dante. He walked around me, taking account of where the suit would need to be tailored. He pulled up the back of my jacket, the pants clearly a tad tight on my behind. "We'll have to blow this part out," he said as I laughed. "Strange expression," I responded. "Yes, I know," he chuckled. "I have to do the same thing on all my suits. Guys like us with the thighs and butt." My soul warmed at the comparison. *He thinks we are similar.* Dante placed a few last-minute pins and ushered me over to the tailor. I didn't enjoy two men staring intently at my body, but it was worth it.

A month later, I was in a perfectly fitted suit standing across from my gorgeous future wife. Two firsts of my lifetime. Lauren and I got married just the two of us on a balcony at Hotel Del Coronado, one of our favorites. My parents and Lauren's younger sister watched from the sand below. The Italians were set to fly out in October for our party. I had convinced Lauren to let me throw a celebration equipped with an open bar, speeches, and an exceptional playlist. It was only fair if we were going to have the private wedding of her dreams. *Marriage is about compromise, right?*

SPILLING THE T

A joyous day

The celebration went off without a hitch, no pun intended, and the next year and a half were spent debating our desire for children. We wavered back and forth constantly on the topic, often sharing our comical "To Child or Not to Child" list with friends. A few of the gems:

PROS	CONS
They will take care of us when we're old	Expensive
We get to share our life wisdom with them	Lack of sleep
They will be adorable and wonderful	We will get sick more
They will say and do funny things	Nice things will be ruined
They will make us happy	We will go to prison for murder if someone mistreats them

We eventually landed on the "To Child" side of the fence and subsequently jumped full force into the task of figuring out how on earth to make baby Bennett a reality. We were excited, although it was painful to revisit the memory of my first disastrous hormone appointment years prior. When I inquired about the effect hormones would have on my ability to pursue children in the future, the doctor had harshly responded, "Your eggs will be scrambled." I left with a pamphlet on egg freezing options, knowing I didn't have the money or emotional wherewithal to go that route. I had to take care of me or else there might have been no me at all. I decided I would worry about children at a later date, and Lauren and I were now at that later date.

While we sat in the kitchen one afternoon discussing our options, I found myself wishing this picture looked different. I didn't regret my decision to not freeze my eggs, but was saddened to face the difficult journey we were surely about to embark on. Having sex to create life seemed like it would be a lot more fun. My wife suddenly interrupted my thought spiral with one simple question, "James, are you sure you can't contribute?" The contradiction hit me like a ton of bricks, leaving me speechless. "Have you actually looked into it?" she pressed on. I wasn't sure how to respond, so I took the next, obvious millennial step and began Googling.

Two months later, my wife and I were sitting across from a local physician who specialized in fertility for transgender couples. "Studies have shown that fertility outcomes for transgender men are in line with that of cisgender women," she said.

"We believe that elevated testosterone levels simply place the processes of ovulation and menstruation into hibernation." My wife and I squeezed hands under the table. Our online search had pointed to this same information, but the prospect didn't feel possible unless it came out of the mouth of an actual healthcare professional. I had preemptively skipped my testosterone shot the night before the appointment just in case. My wife and I didn't have all the facts, but we were sure of one thing. If we were crazy enough to pursue this, I would have to come off hormones.

We marched forward, and after about six weeks of skipped shots, an increase in fatigue, loss in appetite, and an unfortunate resurfacing of distant dysphoria, my testosterone levels resembled those of a typical cisgender woman. It was officially time to begin the "reciprocal IVF" cycle, and I was terrified. The plan was to retrieve my eggs, fertilize them with donor sperm, and hopefully end up with at least three healthy embryos. We would then implant each embryo into my wife and hopefully end up with a baby. Our child would be us with a little help. My egg, "Marco" (our nickname for the donor sperm), and my wife's body to grow the beautiful being(s). We would then use my wife's egg and the same donor for baby number two.

As many cisgender women know, the IVF cycle is not a fun one. It is at least two grueling weeks of self-administered injections into the stomach, almost daily ultrasounds and bloodwork, and an increased feeling of bloating that gets worse by the day. On the day of the "trigger," the anxiety of the upcoming egg retrieval becomes hard to manage. *What if they go in and there are no eggs? What if I've gone through all of this for nothing?* One won't know until they wake up from the procedure.

As I drifted off into anesthesia bliss, I hoped for the best. This had all gone so well, a stark contrast to what I'd been told from the start. I felt optimistic that things might continue in the same vein. I woke up forty-five minutes later to my wife's smiling face and three exclamatory words, proof that my inkling had been correct. "They got ten!" A feeling of joy took over my tired body. We had gone from "scrambled" to "ten." Tears of relief streamed down my cheeks.

The next week and a half were more anxiety-provoking than those prior. My body was crashing from the estrogen high, leaving me unbalanced and uncomfortable, and every two days a call from the embryologist came with an update. It seemed like a far-fetched science experiment, but with each piece of good news, the difficulty began to feel manageable. Our ten eggs turned into eight fertilized embryos, six of which ended up in the "viable" category. Two good, one fair, and three on the border of fair and poor. My wife and I screamed and embraced at the conclusion of each call. One step closer to building our unit.

After one last hurrah, deemed our "hot girl summer" (*ironic, I know*), it was time to put the science to the test. The doctor had us choose from the two "good" embryos, Blue Seven and Red Six. Blue Seven sounded more appealing for whatever reason, and a week or so later, Lauren was on 10mg of Valium with a catheter in her cervix. I watched from across the room as they carefully wheeled in a machine with Blue Seven in a petri dish.

At the invitation from the embryologist, I peered through the microscope at the tiny cluster of cells. I smiled and sat back down while she suctioned the cells out. She then handed the catheter to the doctor, who "implanted" them in a particular part of Lauren's uterus. One final push of air bubbles followed (a way for them to be sure the embryo was in) and that was that.

As the procedure concluded, Lauren was instructed to avoid urinating for at least ten minutes. Poor thing was busting, as they require you to drink an inordinate amount of water forty-five minutes before the procedure. This allows for better visibility of the area where they implant the embryo. I watched as she shifted her weight back and forth on her feet trying to avoid any leakage. My anxiety spiraled in the background with concern that the embryo would fall out. Quite ridiculous in retrospect. Lauren made it almost ten minutes, relieved herself, and we went home.

The next two weeks felt bizarre for me and terrible for Lauren. I had this strange feeling that someone else was there with us, and all she could focus on was the horrendous headache plaguing her existence. Following implant, the potential mother-to-be is required to take daily progesterone pills in order to trick the body into thinking it is pregnant. This way the embryo can be supported in its development. I did all I could to support Lauren as we both anxiously waited for her pregnancy test.

Unfortunately, yet fortunately from the perspective of the current day, the first embryo transfer did not result in pregnancy.

Whether it was an issue at implant or with cell division after implant, we will never know. Looking back though, I feel grateful things happened as they did. I sit here today typing this as my son, Matteo, naps in his nursery. Matteo was conceived in October 2023, a couple months after Blue Seven didn't work out. He is my favorite thing on this earth, and without the failed transfer, he wouldn't be here.

After the stress (and expense) of that first failed embryo transfer, Lauren and I chose to pursue three rounds of IUI instead of a second embryo transfer attempt right away. IUI was less expensive, less taxing on Lauren's body, and our intent was to always try for a baby with her egg and the same donor. The order just differed. Thankfully, against the statistical odds, Lauren got pregnant from the first round of IUI with our only remaining vial of donor sperm from the IVF efforts. We were elated and couldn't wait to meet our precious being. I will never forget the feeling of watching his little heart beat on the ultrasound during one of our first prenatal appointments.

Matteo joined our family nine months later on July 19, 2023, and we've spent his life so far balancing an absurd combination of feelings. I've never felt so happy, stressed, tired, overwhelmed, anxious, and wondrous all at the same time. Parenting with Lauren has solidified our relationship, enhanced our communication, and reminded me of all the reasons I fell in love with her in the first place. I simply could not imagine doing this with anyone else. It is so hard, yet as they say, most definitely worth it.

Our family

Conclusion

As of the current day, my transition feels "complete," or put more aptly, there is nothing much more to be done. I can finally pee standing up after a second failed revision before a successful third. The projection is an issue, but it can still be done. I can mostly navigate social interactions without too much anxiety and although I still struggle, the pain of my remaining dysphoria has gotten exponentially easier to manage over time. I stop myself sooner on the days I catch myself standing in front of the mirror critiquing how curvy my stomach looks or how full my thighs are. I worry less about my height, and I have learned to cease trying on clothes if I'm having one of those days where nothing fits right. I worry less that I don't fit in and remind myself frequently to find connection rather than sit in the feeling that there is no one else like me.

I imagine I will face many more challenges in the future, some I can anticipate and some I can't. I know I'll always have trouble finding men's shoes that fit and will never feel completely comfortable using the men's restroom. I'll always struggle to find men I relate to and never truly master when to come out at work. I'm unsure how I will teach Matteo to use a urinal or when Lauren and I will decide to tell him, and hopefully our other child, that I'm transgender. Regardless, no matter what happens, the reassurance and joy I once lacked now surrounds me in full force. I have James and all the people that helped me find him. Everything else will figure itself out.

I'm not remotely religious or spiritual, but I often daydream of a time in which I am reunited with my former self again. I picture a beautiful field, the two of us sitting together in front of a giant oak tree. The sun is shining, and there is greenery and flowers all around us. Those little white puffballs float through the air, causing both of us to sneeze intermittently. I wrap my arm around her, holding her tight to me. I look down as I compare her legs to mine. So much fuller than mine are now.

"I can't believe how far James and I have come," I tell her. "You won't believe all the things we've been through." She smiles back at me, our eyes meeting in a place of shared love. "I'm so sorry it couldn't be us. You understand, don't you?" I ask as my eyes fill with tears.

"Of course, I do," she says. "We weren't right, and I know that." I squeeze my hand on her shoulder, desperately thanking her with my grasp.

"How funny is it that I ended up with a Lauren?" I ask her, trying to lighten the mood.

"Absolutely hilarious," she responds warmly. "I bet Mom and Dad love that."

I laugh in response. "They sure do. Dad jokes about it every chance he gets."

"I'm sure he does," she chuckles in response.

We both stare off into the distance, embracing the rays of the warm sun. I move my hand from her shoulder down to her hand. I hold it tight, using my other hand to wipe my wet cheeks.

"There's simply not enough words in the world to thank you," I tell her.

She squeezes my hand back. "You don't have to."

I look down. "I just wouldn't be here without everything you did to get me here. All of the pain, isolation, and insecurity you faced to introduce me to James," I say.

She looks back at me. "It was all worth it," she says with a smile.

We sit together for hours, sharing many more tears and laughs. We talk of all the hilarious experiences and all the horrendously painful ones. She teases me for the silly things I said and did when I was deep in the thick of transition. We look at pictures and reminisce over all that has happened since she left. I tell her how much I've missed her, and she responds that she's missed me too. We both acknowledge how necessary it was for her to leave. As the sun goes down, we eventually get up and embrace each other one last time. We say one final goodbye and she is gone once again. "I love you, Lauren," I say as she disappears. "Thank you for everything."

Acknowledgments

Although this book is already dedicated to my mom, dad, and Lauren, I would like to take this opportunity to thank them here as well. Mom and dad, thank you from the bottom of my heart for the unconditional love, patience, and endless support you've given me over the years. I simply would not be here without you. Lauren, thank you for choosing me, encouraging me, and loving me through all the emotional ups and downs of both writing this book and living through most of the events in it. I could not have found a better life partner and there is not a day that goes by in which I don't feel grateful.

To my family and friends, especially those who took the time to respond to my prompts, thank you for seeing me, supporting me, and never once judging me. I am fortunate beyond words to have so many beautiful souls in my life. And to Aaron, thank you for drawing the amazing hand!

To my precious Matteo, thank you for making me a dad. I love you and I look forward to the day I can share this with you. I promise to always be there for you the way my family and friends have been for me, no matter what.

To my sweet corgi, Bailee, you can't read, but thank you for the cuddles through the tears, surgery recoveries, and bad days. You will never know how much you mean to me.

And to you, the reader, thank you for keeping an open mind and allowing me the opportunity to share my journey. The thought of anything I've written resonating with any one of you warms my heart in a way that I can't describe. Life can be so isolating and to be understood in any capacity is such a gift.

About the Author

JAMES BENNETT is a thirty-five-year-old trans man from Australia, currently living in San Diego, California. He works in the medical device industry and is happily married with a son, a grumpy old corgi, and someday soon, hopefully another baby (fingers crossed). He loves cycling, traveling, and writing. James felt the world needed this book as he grew tired of people asking about his genitals, yet is also not convinced they know why they shouldn't.

www.ingramcontent.com/pod-product-compliance
Lightning Source LLC
Chambersburg PA
CBHW030517080526
44586CB00011B/225